Praise for *The Authentic Salesman*

"Michael McIntyre is truly the authentic salesman. It's so refreshing in a world of egos and chest-pounding that an author can be both vulnerable and helpful. This book will give you immediate takeaways that can impact you both personally and professionally. After all, we are all in sales!"

—Tommy Spaulding
Author of the *New York Times* bestseller *It's Not Just Who You Know*

"McIntyre is the quintessential salesman. He used his natural skills and learned techniques to pull himself up from rags to a classic example of American success. In this book, *The Authentic Salesman*, he teaches the techniques we can all use to follow in his footsteps."

—Michael Gorton
CEO, Principal Solar

"If you're in sales, you owe it to yourself to buy this book. Michael, a seasoned veteran, shares his lifelong love of sales by providing practical lessons that will greatly enhance your results. Once we recognize that sales is truly a process, we can use his proven techniques to build a skillset that few people have in their possession. *The Authentic Salesman* is an excellent learning guide, and the author's thoughtful and pragmatic approach to sales will help you both in your career and daily life."

—Brian O. Casey
CEO, Westwood Holdings Group

"Michael McIntyre imparts important lessons about life and success in *The Authentic Salesman*. His insights, knowledge, and experiences are immensely valuable to people ranging from those new to selling to experienced professionals—and to those seeking to better understand the successful entrepreneurial mindset. This book contains a lot of clear, practical advice and is entertaining to read. Michael's messages about the importance of hard work, the willingness and ability to learn, knowing your product, and understanding the client and letting them be right are universal keys to success in virtually all service and sales businesses. He has set his goals in life high and has achieved them through courage, focus, and relentless attention to the practices he shares in his book."

—Daniel L. Butcher
Managing partner, Strasburger & Price, LLP

"Being a surgeon for over thirty years, I have worked with a multitude of talented and gifted people with large personalities. It has been a privilege to have been trained by truly gifted and brilliant surgeons in the world; however good they may be, though, they generally have not necessarily acquired the art of listening—or selling, for that matter. We are in a new paradigm with more elective surgeries being done now than ever before; the medical landscape is changing rapidly in our country. Michael makes an excellent point about 'active listening' that really caught my attention and, I believe, can make a significant difference in improving any relationship—doctor and patient, parent and child, or vendor and consumer. Whatever the relationship, we can all learn something valuable from Michael's insights."

—Michel Stephan, MD, FACS

"Developing a strategy that works is difficult. Belief in your strategy is more challenging, but implementing the whole package is the hardest thing to accomplish. Michael has what it takes: a strategy, belief in it, experience, failures to learn from, and the persistence and energy that have led to amazing success. This book brings the art and science of sales to life and provides the newbie and veteran alike with exceedingly great value."

—Mark A. Palmer, DDS

THE
AUTHENTIC
SALESMAN

THE
AUTHENTIC
SALESMAN

Mastering the Art

of Transforming

Real Objections

into Real Transactions

Michael McIntyre

BB BROWN BOOKS small press

The Authentic Salesman
Mastering the Art of Transforming Real Objections into Real Transactions

Brown Books Small Press
16250 Knoll Trail Drive, Suite 205
Dallas, Texas 75248
BrownBooksSmallPress.com
(972) 381-0009

ISBN 978-1-61254-764-0
Library of Congress Control Number 2011927151

Printed in the United States of America
10 9 8 7 6 5 4 3 2 1

For more information, please visit TheAuthenticSalesman.com

This book is dedicated to my wife,
Stacye, and to my late father-in-law, Jack.

To Stacye: Like a saint, Stacye patiently
allowed me to be "in the zone"
for hours on end and was always
understanding of my crazy mood swings.
Stacye provided me with the honest feedback
that only a loving wife can give,
letting me share a very difficult part of our life.
I love this beautiful brunette very much
and love being married to her.

To Jack: He was a real "man's man."
More importantly, he was the best coach and
father any son-in-law could wish for.
I love and miss him very much.

Contents

Part 4: The Presentation

Part 5: After the Sale

Foreword

I met Michael for the first time in early 2005 at the Young Presidents' Organization (YPO). We were both members of YPO, an organization that connects successful young chief executives in a global network. Founded in 1950 in New York City by Ray Hickok, the organization unites approximately eighteen thousand business leaders in more than one hundred countries around a shared mission: Better Leaders Through Education and Idea Exchange. As a YPO forum member, I've come to regard Michael not only as a masterful salesman but a close friend as well.

As I read this book, I discovered this was not just another "how-to" book on sales. It was much more than that: it's a book written by a guy who lives and breathes selling. I believe in the saying, "You can't teach what you don't know, and you can't lead where you won't go." When it comes to selling . . . Michael can teach and lead it all day long.

In this book, we see firsthand the up and down nature of sales through Michael's eyes. We are exposed to the life lessons that shaped and molded his philosophies and created his success. When it comes to sales, you are either good at it or you are not. There is no in-between. But salesmanship is also an art that the good ones are always perfecting. You need to be constantly educating yourself and working toward making yourself better, and the principles Michael sets down here are spot-on.

I agree with his statement that you are always selling somebody something. Let's face it, everybody is in sales—no matter who you are, no matter what you're doing. I believe that wholeheartedly. Organizations need that message to come straight from the top. Everyone in the organization must know what you're selling and how to sell it the right way. It doesn't matter if you're in accounting, legal, or marketing. Everyone is selling the corporate mantra. If they know it, they can sell it. It's a team approach.

But being able to function as a team doesn't just happen—it takes work. I believe a high-quality sales team needs to go through extensive training. Most of the time you get one shot at a sale. It is a percentage game. You can't afford to burn any leads.

Being prepared is essential. In law school, I was taught never to ask a question in the courtroom I did not know the answer to. This is also essential in sales. We rehearse, or "role play," countless hours in preparation for each sale. By putting yourself in the shoes of the person you are going to be selling to, you are able to anticipate the questions, objections, or concerns that they may bring up.

There is no one who respects the art of salesmanship more than our family. The wonderful thing about America is that it was built by great salesmen. It's part of the American dream. You've got to respect it, especially when you've lived it your whole life. There truly is an art to selling, and we believe in that art form.

You have to sense the fluidity of selling. It's not black and white. In many ways, it's intuitive. You need to be able to think on your feet and see an opening—and when it presents itself, you need to go for it with no hesitation. My father routinely gives speeches to our sales team and to our clients. During these speeches, at one point or another, he'll trot out a truly great line: "There are five parts to a sale, and number one is 'ask for the order.' I've forgotten the other four." It always gets a laugh—but it's true. You've got to ask for the order.

This book is just like Michael McIntyre the man: genuine and vulnerable, yet in firm possession of what it takes to make a sale. In these pages, he shows a real willingness to open himself up. He arms you with his life's lessons so you can take on the sea of troubles called sales. He's sharing his story in hopes that you will learn both from his successes and his failures.

I hope you enjoy *The Authentic Salesman* as much as I did.

—Jerry Jones Jr.
Executive Vice President/Chief Sales and Marketing Officer
Dallas Cowboys Football Club

Preface

I wrote this book because I *love* to pay it forward by coaching and training. I am at my best when I am helping people prosper. I truly enjoy taking a newbie and turning them into a success, or taking a veteran on the verge of burnout and relighting their candle.

When I told friends and business associates that I was writing a book, they would look at me and say, "Dude, how are you doing that? Man, I could never write a book." This always shocked me.

For me, it was just a matter of sitting down at the computer and beginning to write. The words just came out of me. It truly wasn't difficult—it was a blast. When I wrote, time would totally stand still for me; I would sit down and not get up for hours. However, having to relive some of the dark places in my career and life in order to write about them wasn't fun. I didn't want to write just a how-to book; I really wanted the reader to get a sense of the situation. Life is about change, risk, success, failure, and even death. I think it's very good to explore and reflect—not to get stuck, however, but to learn and move on.

When I wrote this, two major things happened for me. One was that I sold my company. Though this was not at all a bad thing, at the age of forty-seven, it wasn't a great thing, either. The question became, "What's next?" The other thing that was and still is hugely profound for me was that I accepted Jesus Christ as my Lord and Savior. Now, you must know this: if you were to have told me that a year prior, I would have laughed in your face and dismissed you as a nutjob. Yet by the Grace of God, I am a Christ Follower. I wasn't an atheist by any means; I was more of an "all roads lead to Rome" kind of guy. It is a big stretch for me to reveal all that I have shared in this book. I know it's my faith that allowed me to do this—to be authentic and vulnerable.

In this book, you will learn that a guy from Flint, Michigan, without a pedigree, any money, contacts, family favors, or a chance *can* make a difference in his business, family, and community. The truth is, I have learned more from my failures than I have from any of my successes . . . maybe because I have so many more failures.

Enjoy the read.

—Michael

Acknowledgments

First I must say thank you to my wife, Stacye. To say that she helped with this book is an understatement. Not only did Stacye listen, make suggestions, read, and edit, she also allowed me to share some difficult times in her life. Having to relive those times wasn't a walk in the park, but she graciously did so without reservation, giving me confidence and love.

I want to acknowledge my three beautiful daughters, Brittany, Brianna, and Brecca, who encourage me by example. They are dedicated and disciplined young ladies who inspire me constantly. Watching them grow in their faith is truly awesome.

My brother, Matt, has been instrumental in my becoming a Christ Follower. Matt truly walks the walk in his faith and always gives me words of wisdom.

To my mother, who gave me the gift of forgiveness and commitment, and to my father, who passed on to me the gift of perseverance.

I have several friends who helped me with this journey, one of whom is Jerry Jones Jr., who recently amazed me by quoting some paragraphs from the book. I know he put in huge amounts of time working on his foreword, and I so appreciate it. He is a sincere and good friend.

To Brian Casey, Tommy Spaulding, Dan Butcher, and Dr. Mark Palmer, who gave of their valuable time and endorsements.

My buddies Greg Anderson, Matt Levy, Peter Gudmundsson, David McGuire, Barron Fletcher, Stephen Rogers, and Eric VandenBranden, who listened with great patience to my ups and downs throughout this process.

To my staff, Matt Sowards and Ron Richey, who helped in many ways behind the scenes—from fixing my computer to helping with rewrites and any and everything else.

Michael Gorton, who actually read all the versions of the book (God bless you) and was very generous with his time and suggestions.

Dr. Mike Stephan, a medical genius and great friend who believes that I can do anything. Thanks for all your encouragement and friendship.

To my good friend Chris Klienert, who took precious time to help edit the book. You are amazing in your generosity.

Finally to my publisher, Cynthia Stillar, a publishing genius who is amazing at dealing with authors. A special thank you to Omar Mediano, a web genius, and to Auburn Layman and Ian Birnbaum, my brilliant editors at Brown Books Small Press in Dallas.

Thank you to God, from whom all blessings flow.

Part 1

Everybody Sells

one

---- -- -- -- -- ----

You're in Sales. Yes, You.

Doctors must heal, artists must draw, singers must sing, and preachers must preach. Actors act, teachers teach, and all are a part of the great wide world of sales. No matter what your occupation, I promise you are always selling something—most of the time not as well as you could be. I often hear people say, "Man, that guy could sell ice to an Eskimo." Well, that's a good thing, I suppose, especially if the Eskimo was in need of ice. The sales profession is an amazing one, but even if you're not in direct sales, this book will still help you. In the end, no matter what occupation you pursue, we are all sales people on one level or another. I know that better sales skills will help you be more successful in your profession.

I hear a lot of people say, "I'm an engineer; I leave all that sales stuff to the sales guys." Or, "I work in the lab and do research. I leave all the marketing to the marketing team and drug reps." Do you really believe that? Let me tell you, it's not entirely true. You are still selling something to someone, even if you're just selling your team on your ideas.

Careers in sales can be challenging, yet at the same time they can be very lucrative for the dedicated and driven sales professional. After all, where would we be if sales hadn't been made? Do you really think Columbus would have sailed if he had an actuary or an accountant make the presentation to the Queen about discovering the New World? Can you just hear it now? "Oh yes, Your Majesty, according to my calculations, the chances are probably less than 50 percent that I will discover anything on this expensive voyage, and your money will probably be lost. It looks really risky." What about city skyscrapers or the automobile? Can you hear Henry Ford having one of his brilliant engineers try to explain why they only offered one color of the Model T? If we left it to an engineer, it might have sounded something like this: "We are very sorry; the only paint pigment we can economically and efficiently produce is black. This will also keep the replacement parts more readily available, since we calculate you will need to replace them over a dozen times within the first one thousand miles of driving." *Ouch!* A great salesman once said this instead: "Mr. Prospect, you can have this fine Model T in any color you wish, as long as it is black." Now, doesn't that sound better? It is simple, funny, direct, and to the point.

The fact is that we need salespeople. Ronald Reagan was truly one of the best. He would look you right in the eye (through the camera) and speak to you in that charismatic voice, as he so eloquently did when he addressed the nation in his infamous March 1987 speech dealing with the Iran-Contra affair:

> Now what should happen when you make a mistake is this: you take your knocks, you learn your lessons,

and then you move on. That's the healthiest way to deal with a problem. . . . You know, by the time you reach my age, you've made plenty of mistakes. And if you've lived your life properly—so, you learn. You put things in perspective. You pull your energies together. You change. You go forward.

He would say it with a smile and sound completely honest, and we loved it.

A presidential analogy of the opposite effect comes in the form of Jimmy Carter. He simply was not a good salesperson, though he was very academic. He looked you right in the eye and said, "We have an energy crisis; turn your thermostat to sixty-eight degrees and freeze to death while the oil companies get rich." This was less inspiring. Of course, he didn't say it quite that way, but that's the way many people interpreted it. His delivery was bad. Reagan was positive, upbeat, and smiling; he made us believe we could win.

This is a book about the art of sales. There are a lot of life lessons in here as well. Some are hard to learn, some not so hard—all are relevant. If you allow it, the tools in this book will dramatically increase your closing percentages and may even provide you with some insights into life and business, along with a laugh or two.

two

Selling Anyone on Anything

The biggest hurdle to get through when you are selling is asking for the order. Many times we make up things in our minds like, "No way can I approach them with this." Or, "I would never ask for that in this situation." This begs the question: Why not? You already have a no, so why not improve on it—or at least try?

A few years ago my wife and I were shopping at Neiman Marcus (a high-end retailer). We were looking at several items, and I said this to the salesperson while we were picking things out: "We would like to buy all of this, but I really need to get a decent discount on this purchase." At that moment, my wife stopped in her tracks and looked at me as if I just pulled out a gun with the intention of robbing the place. I did not acknowledge my wife's expression; I just continued to look at the sales rep. Without hesitation she said, "Let me go ask the manager, I will be right back."

My wife was amazed that they didn't call store security and have us thrown out—after all, this was Neiman Marcus and they have a reputation to uphold. Three minutes later, the sales rep came back with a nice simile on her face and said, "We can offer you a 5 percent discount for customer loyalty."

I came right back and said, "Thank you. However, we really were looking for 10 percent."

"OK," she said. "If you take all these items, we can accommodate you."

My wife was shocked. To be honest, I was little surprised, too. But what the heck—we saved a decent amount of money, and they made the sale. Some may say that's more of a negotiating story; true enough, but negotiations are sales, too. The point is to ask; you *never* know what the answer may be!

Being able to have a company give you the top commission contract is a good thing and sometimes is not easy. However, getting them to pay for your marketing campaigns in addition to that is quite another matter. I learned early in my experience with running a sales organization that *actual* production screams louder than any claim you make about what you're *going* to produce. Most manufactures hear from the distribution company about how much they can produce, but few actually deliver. It comes down to the old adage, "The proof is in the pudding." It really is—talkers talk and doers do!

For example, in 1996, after my insurance agency had a pretty good production quarter under its belt—which was accomplished purely because of our ability, marketing ingenuity, and the grace of God—we had the desire to get bigger. However, we needed a lot of capital to accomplish that. I really didn't want any partners, so I decided to go ask for the order in a different way: directly.

I went to the two companies I was selling for and asked for the money to expand our mailings. We needed $100,000 per month. (That's right, 100K per month!) This was 1996, and direct mail was the best way for us to get our leads. It was expensive but very effective. I presented the need to both companies, and not only did we get the money, we also engineered it with them so that we didn't have to pay it back. My staff just shook their heads in disbelief. One of them said, "Michael, how did you get this done?"

I replied, "I asked for it and they said yes."

The fact is, we could have made it without the money. It would have caused much slower growth, but we would have made it. I knew that if I got a no, it wouldn't be the end of the world. However, it was truly a win–win for all. They received a ton of good production, and we could do a ton of direct mailing and lower our expenses.

Even the Small Stuff is Sellable

I was in Scottsdale, Arizona, one night in 1997, having an important business dinner at an upscale restaurant. It became readily apparent that the waitstaff was really off their mark. There were six of us at the table, and it was beginning to get a little uncomfortable. I excused myself and went to have a private conversation with our waiter.

As I approached him I said, "Excuse me, I am sorry to bother you, I know you're very busy. However, I was just talking to my associates and we were wondering if you had a unique compensation package." He looked at me a little perplexed, so I proceeded. "I was curious to know if you work on salary as a waiter. Or do you work for tips?"

Immediately he got it and apologized for his behavior; he changed on a dime. We went on to have a great experience, and he received a very nice tip. Win–win. The point is that you can turn any situation into a sellable situation by creating a slight paradigm shift in the way people look at things.

Ask and You Shall Receive . . .

One afternoon in 1996 I was in Des Moines, Iowa, having just had a lunch meeting with the CEO and executive staff of the insurance company for which we were selling. They were a relatively new company with some very experienced management. We had a good contract with them, and they were trying to get their new company off of the ground. Our desire was to develop new products and give them more sales; they were very eager to meet with us. I had a great rapport with the CEO—he was "old-school" and so was I. He would always do as he promised; in the insurance business, believe it or not, that was a rare thing. So I decided to bring my executive team to meet their executive staff—in all, there were ten of us.

The company had picked us up at the airport with two limos. I rode in the front one with the CEO and his assistant; we were driving back to the airport after lunch when he said, "Michael, I need more production from you. I need $100 million a year in production."

I replied by saying, "OK, I can do that, but I would like one hundred thousand stock options."

"I can't do that," he said, "I haven't done that with any of the other distribution companies."

"This is true," I said. "However, none of them can deliver what I can."

Keep in mind that this was all happening while we were driving down the interstate, heading back to the airport. He ordered his driver to pull over and stop, which the driver did. There we were—two limos on the side of the interstate, stopped.

He then turned to me and said, "Damn it, Michael, you got a deal." We shook hands and he got out, walked back to the other limo right behind us, and got in. My people got out of that limo and joined me off to the airport. That deal was one of the biggest in my career. It took about ten minutes, and I only overcame one objection.

No matter where you are, be ready for a sale—even in a limo parked on the shoulder of the interstate.

Part 1
Homework

――――――― ―――――――

What is it that you're selling? Is it a product? A service? Your expertise or experience? What is it that you have that other people are willing to pay for?

Whatever that is, it's your "product." Now that you know your product, list its selling points below.

Selling Points

―――――――――――――――――――――――――――――――――

―――――――――――――――――――――――――――――――――

―――――――――――――――――――――――――――――――――

―――――――――――――――――――――――――――――――――

What possible objections do you think people will have to buying your product? Are there any aspects of the product that people don't think they need?

Possible Objections

―――――――――――――――――――――――――――――――――

―――――――――――――――――――――――――――――――――

―――――――――――――――――――――――――――――――――

―――――――――――――――――――――――――――――――――

How can you tackle those objections?

Your Rebuttals

_____

_____

_____

_____

Part 2

Proven Sales Techniques

three

———— — — — — ————

The Five-Point Close

Whatever career path you choose, you must have the right tools to succeed. Some companies will help you gain these tools, while others will expect you to come to the game fully equipped. Wherever you work, the skills that you have already developed will be highly appreciated, as will your willingness and ability to learn those things you don't know—and to do so quickly. If you are in sales, those skills and tools will be even more important because you may be out your own or be responsible for meeting your personal goals.

"Tools like what?" you may ask. Well, first you need a legal pad. This will allow you to take more notes while you are dealing with your colleagues or clients. These notes will come in handy; if you don't have them, you will wish you did. You will also need a good black-ink pen with ink that shows clearly. You may have heard of "the power of the pen." It is one of the most effective tools in selling, no matter what your product. You will also need extra pens; having one for each prospect plus several extras is a good idea.

One of the all-time greatest closes is with the pen. You give your prospect a direct close, fill out the paperwork, say, "We need you to OK this, Mr. Prospect," and hand them your pen. They will take it. If they don't use it right away (within thirty to sixty seconds), say, "Pardon me," take the pen back (gently, of course), scribble on your legal pad to make sure that it works, look at it, and hand it back to the prospect without saying anything. Nine times out of ten they will use it, assuming your presentation was good and it is a product that they feel they can use. The power of the pen is great.

Another tool is your briefcase or bag—but only if you have it organized to the utmost degree. No one wants to deal with disorganized people, even if they are disorganized themselves. Have your applications under the third page of your legal pad and have some of the prospect's information filled out before you meet them. This shows that you are professional and that you fully expected they would take advantage of this great product.

The above are just the physical, basic items that you need. There are many other tools that you will need to have or be familiar with in order to be successful; among those might be in-depth presentations, knowledge of your facts, a laptop with relevant PowerPoint presentations, graphs, samples, the Internet, third-party articles, celebrity endorsements, and so forth. These can be extremely useful. You should know your product inside and out, whether it's an insurance policy, a Cadillac, a G5 jet, or a vacuum cleaner. If you are working with a PowerPoint presentation or a flip chart, know it thoroughly. Rehearse it, and then rehearse it again. Look at your sales presentation as if you are going to be the lead in a Broadway play—you *must* know your lines! However, be sure that you are not reading in a monotone voice directly from your presentation. Make eye contact, vary your tone, and show that you are interested in the prospect and their needs and that you believe in your product.

The Five-Point Close is a very basic but dynamic sales technique with proven results. Yet when salespeople are trained on this process, sometimes even the very sophisticated salesperson doesn't get it. They wish to hold on to their beliefs; they want and need to be right. To those people we say, "You're right. Your way is better for you, but just for kicks, let's compare closing percentages—or better yet, let's compare 1099s." As Ronald Reagan once said, "Facts are stubborn things." They are indisputable.

The truth is in the bottom line. Either your technique is working and helping you make the money you want to make . . . or it's not. The Five-Point Close works for me, and I have seen it work for many others. If you follow the Five-Point Close, you will sell everyone as long as they have two things: the need and the money.

Point One: Let Them Be Right!

One of the biggest mistakes salespeople make is to allow their ego to drive their actions during a meeting. When we emotionally invest in the process of the presentation, our first rejection can punish our egos, and we're devastated and act accordingly.

Picture this scenario: You arrive at your prospect's house five minutes early, you receive a terrific greeting, and you think to yourself, *Great, they want me here.* You warm up with the prospect. You move to the kitchen table and seat Mr. and Mrs. Prospect in the correct positions and proceed ever-so-eloquently to make a fantastic presentation. You share some laughs as well as some serious emotions with the prospect and feel pretty good. In fact, you are starting to count your commissions (a fatal mistake) and you go for the oldest close in the book, the assumptive close. It sounds something like this: "OK, Mr. Prospect, now that you see how great this product/service is, do you want that sent to your home or to your office?" Or, "OK, Mr. and Mrs. Prospect, you folks are smart people and you see the obvious value here. How do you spell your middle name?" What happens next is very common. The prospect declares their intention to think on the proposal or to consult a trusted advisor, or they may even remark on the expense of the product. At this point you are thinking, *The prospect is saying no to me personally!*

Here's what you do: agree with them! That's correct; let them be right. It doesn't matter what their objection is, simply agree with it. Human nature dictates that 99 percent of us have a very powerful need to be right. Accepting the consequences for being wrong is tough, so most of us want to be right. Think about the arguments we get into with our children, spouses, parents, coworkers, and governments. We all think we are right, but the fact is, we cannot all be right. Someone must be wrong. Use this to your advantage. In a professional situation, we often have little emotional attachment, which makes it much easier to allow your prospect to be right.

If you think that your prospect needs to be right in order to feel good about making a purchase, let them be right. You are there to make a sale and improve their life in some fashion. You will not be able to help them if you insist on being right. Bear in mind that the prospect may have had more training than you have had.

For example, imagine that your prospect is fifty years old and has been married for twenty-five years. Over the years, this couple has probably heard at least three hundred presentations together and countless more on their own. Remember, a sales presentation can be made anywhere; you do not have to be sitting at the kitchen table in your home to receive a sales presentation. You could be buying a car, shopping for a suit, or looking at houses.

As a salesperson, the conversation that will lose you the sale when your ego is involved goes something similar to this:

Prospect: We really have to think about this, Michael. We don't make any snap decisions.

Ego-salesman: I just thoroughly and honestly explained everything about this product/service. What on earth could you want to think about? In fact, Mr. Prospect, you'd better sign this tonight, because you never know if this product/service will be available at this price again.

As an "ego-salesperson," you have just put a lot of pressure on the prospect to make them feel as if they need to do something now or miss the chance to purchase the product/service. On top of that, you've now told your prospect that they are wrong. Putting pressure on your client to sign when they are teetering is a sure way to make them decide not to buy at that moment. You've fallen into the stereotype of a pushy salesperson—and no one wants to deal with a pushy salesperson.

What it all boils down to is that your prospect has a reason to say no. You might be able to stun them with your facts and figures and logically you could be spot-on, but if you insist on being right, you will be—and broke as well! You may have won the battle, but you will have lost the war. You can be right some of the time but never all of the time. What is more important to you—being right or putting food on your table, gas in your automobile, and a roof over your head?

Agreeing with objections is a very important aspect of the Five-Point Close. First of all, expect objections. Eighty-nine percent of sales first come with an objection. Twenty percent of salespeople are responsible for 80 percent of sales because they can get past the objection and not take it personally. When your prospect wants to take time to think or get advice from someone else, respond by saying, "You're right; you should think about it or talk to your advisor." When you do this, you will open up a big window of opportunity, because you will be doing something that few salespeople take the time to do: you will be listening and valuing your prospect's concerns and questions. When you let them be right and show some vulnerability, your prospects will be able to better relate to you and magical things will happen to your sales

When this window of opportunity opens, you must jump through it immediately. The way you speak to your prospect during the open-window moment—which is just after you have agreed with your prospect's objection—is very important and crucial to the success of your sale.

Point Two: Overcome the Objection

Once someone has given you an objection and told you that you're wrong, telling them they are right triggers quite a conversation. However, the prospect may be so used to hearing the ego-salesman's battle cry that they may not have heard you. So repeat your agreement with their objection. The conversation may sound like this:

Prospect: Well, Michael, Mary and I have never made a decision on the spot without sleeping on it. We have always done that and always will. But thanks just the same. We will let you know.

Me: I agree, Mr. Prospect. You should sleep on it and think about it. It's a big decision.

Now, at this point your prospect will do one of two things: He may come back and say, "No, Michael, it sounds good, but we still need time to think about it," or he might look a little perplexed and say, "Yes, you're right, we need to think about it."

You just got the prospect to agree with you! You need to let that resonate in the air for a couple of seconds. You will hear your window opening. That's your opportunity to go to the second point of the Five-Point Close: overcoming the objection.

Once you have agreed with Mr. and Mrs. Prospect that they need time to think about the decision, let them do so. If you are in their house, look straight into their eyes and say, "I'll be back in five minutes. I must make a call to check in." At this point, get up and leave the room. Preferably you can go to your car and call your sales manager, check in with your spouse, or take a five-minute break. I like to go to my car, get some more sales material, and make a few calls. It is important that the prospects know they can speak openly without you overhearing their conversation. Even when you are addressing only one person, leaving him or her alone may still be beneficial—trust your instincts and your experience to let you know what should be done.

Once you come back into their space, you need to sit down and see the lay of the land. If the objection is money, agree with them again: "I agree, Mr. Prospect, it is a lot of money, but money is not your problem—it is the solution to your problem." Let that resonate in the air for a couple of seconds.

If their objection is that they don't know you or your company, respond with something along the lines of, "I agree, we are strangers; our company hasn't heard of you either." (A little levity is good.) "However, I am here to introduce us and let you get familiar with our company. Mr. Prospect, we should take the time to get to know one another." This time is spent overcoming the objection. In essence, when you agree with the prospect's objection, you have your window to jump through.

If you have left the client's space and come back into the room, sit down and start to write on your order form or application. You are assuming the sale and you need to get information from the client.

Overcoming objections is fun and easy once you practice it. For some people it will be very natural; for others it will take a little more effort to make it work smoothly. Practice makes perfect, and while you may not get it right the first time, each time you miss a sale you will learn something that will help you get it right more often.

If your prospect agrees with everything you say, watch out for the "yes, yes, bomb." These folks have most likely figured out a long time ago that you can agree your way into not buying anything. When I detect a "yes, yes, bomb," I stop my presentation and ask a question: "Mr. and Mrs. Prospect, you obviously see the value of this product, and you seem to like everything I am saying. Do you have this product/service now?" Their "yes, yes, bomb" response is usually something along the lines of, "Oh, no we don't. We get all our product/services from our friend, relative, or coworker. We were just curious about how much yours cost or how it was different."

At that point, unless they are not happy with the product/service they are getting or they are angry with the person that they are buying from, you will do better to save your time and leave. That is not to say that you should give up in the face of competition. I am saying that if someone is emotionally tied to a product/service through a loved one, you are going to have a tough time getting that prospect to buy from you. On rare occasions, you will come across a prospect who really likes your product/service, wants it at first blush, and doesn't offer any objections—however, these are rare. Why did you get an appointment from people who have no intention to buy in the first place? You got the appointment because the prospect likes to be accommodating and they say yes to nearly everything.

What happens when the objection seems insurmountable? You still follow the Five-Point Close and overcome it. Too often we project our own doubts and insecurities into situations. I call this "making it up." This brings out self-doubt and unnecessary anxiety.

When I first started in the sales profession, I was always afraid of the classic objection, "Sounds good, but I want to think about it." To deal with this, I created an atmosphere in my presentation that eliminated that objection 90 percent of the time.

After the warm-up, right after you sit down at the kitchen table, say, "Mr. and Mrs. Prospect, I am going to share some very interesting and beneficial ideas with you. I have some nice illustrations and facts and figures that are very important. But first I want to show you this piece of paper. You can see there is nothing on this paper except for these blank lines that represent nothing. There is nothing that can't easily be explained or anything that is unique, convoluted, or distracting. Mr. and Mrs. Prospect, when I finish with my presentation, I promise you will understand my idea/product/service as easily as you understand this blank piece of paper. I only have one favor to ask of you: by the time we are all finished here today, I would appreciate a yes or no answer. Is that fair enough?"

Two things can happen at this point. They will either agree that it is a fair request or say that they never make an on-the-spot decision. Knowing where you stand and what sort of objection you may have to conquer later is a big advantage. It is so much easier to win the war when you know how to strategically plan for the battle. Most people will want to be "fair" and will agree. You still may get some pushback at the close, but you have already addressed it so you have the answers that they need to hear to close the deal.

The other objection most salespeople fear is money. You can also eliminate this one up front with several questions and some investigation. One key indication is the kind of car a prospect drives—although you should take this with a grain of salt, as sometimes the car will reflect preference rather than bank balances. Overcome objections before or as soon as they start. This will greatly increase your closing ratio and will make the process much more fun for you and your prospect.

What Happens When You Get a No?

You cannot let a prospect just say no without any explanation. If you do, you're stuck. You must dig for the objection. You might say, "OK, I understand, Mr. Prospect, now could you tell me what you mean by that?" They then might say, "I mean no! It is much too expensive." Or, "I mean no, I have to think about this." Or they may say, "I have to talk with my stock broker before I do this." Whatever they say, you agree with them; remember, let them be right. You can then go straight into the rest of the Five-Point Close.

The point here is that a successful salesperson doesn't simply accept a no—they dig for the objection. Start asking questions about the no and sooner or later you will find the reasons behind the objection. Be careful how you phrase the "digging" question so that you get the maximum amount of information. "What I hear you saying, Mr. Prospect, is that you don't want to reduce taxes on your income." Or, "What I hear you saying is that you don't want to buy a new house." This will flush out their objection and give you something to latch on to, after which you can go right back into your Five-Point Close.

Point Three: Provide a Selling Point

After you get the objection, you must agree with it, overcome it, and then implement point three—provide a strong selling point. This is for your prospect's benefit; it gives him or her a reason to buy from such an agreeable, smart person. It is human nature to associate with people like ourselves, and those are also the people with whom we wish to do business. If someone agreed with you and gave you valuable information to make your life cheaper, safer, faster, or more pleasant, why wouldn't you do business with them?

So you say, "I agree, Mr. Prospect, it is a lot of money." Then pause briefly and continue, "However, money is not your problem—it is the solution to your problem." Pause again and then say, "And as you know, this policy will protect your family from an untimely death, and if you live for the next twenty years, look at what you can accumulate, tax deferred!"

You could also try saying something to the effect of, "I agree, Mr. Prospect. This is a new company, and you really don't know us at all. I was skeptical myself, but I did my due diligence and checked out the company, front to back, and I found that while it is a newer company, they are also innovative with their products, like the one I showed you here tonight. You can get a nice bonus and a great rate locked in for at least twelve months. After the twelve months, we can reevaluate your position and make sure it is going well."

Remember, you must know what your product really offers your prospect. Why should the prospect buy this from you? Make a list. Some companies spend large sums of money touting the benefits of their product or service. Your company's training seminars are great opportunities to learn all of the positive attributes of your product or service, even if it may cost you a few dollars to attend. Most sales organizations also have a mentoring program, and it is up to you to get with an experienced sales rep and ask those questions to which you need the answers. Go to the heart of the business and ask questions. You will learn from these people, and it will help you become financially secure.

Write down all the benefits of your product on three-by-five index cards, one benefit per card, and commit them to memory. When necessary, recite these benefits in a way that evokes emotion and passion. Most people will buy on emotion rather than logic. You can sometimes have two strong selling points—but never more than that. If you give them three great benefits, you are providing too many things to think about. Remember the blank piece of paper? It is simple and understandable—keep it that way.

OK, we have agreed with the prospect's objection, overcome it, and given a strong selling point or two—now what? Be silent. As we say in sales lingo, "Shut up and stay shut up!" However, if they look at you at any time and say, "Hey, Michael, you know what—I get it. Sign me up," don't say, "OK, but first I have two more points to get to." Start writing the order!

Point Four: Create a Sense of Urgency

From the time you have an appointment you need to create a sense of urgency, but do it in a way that never makes the prospect feel rushed or hurried. You can do this in subtle and not-so-subtle ways. Below is an example:

"Mr. Prospect, I am out here today speaking with many people like you. In fact, I have several appointments in this area over the next couple of days, and it's important that you take advantage of my time while I am here. I'm at your service now and I am very happy to be able to share some very good ideas with you. I want to show you a piece of paper. . . ."

Early in my career, my manager explained to me that he never did callbacks because they so rarely paid off. They created uncertainty about his income for the week, and he felt his time was better spent chasing new leads. His words, and seeing his reasoning in action, made a lot of sense to me. It is good advice and (though I know that there are legitimate reasons to make callbacks) if you stick to your convictions, you will make more sales now.

Many people say you shouldn't pressure someone into buying. My response to that is, "I don't believe any of us are that powerful." You can never pressure someone into doing something; people can only pressure themselves. You cannot force someone to love you, and in the same way, you cannot force someone to buy. If we could, we would all be millionaires.

A sense of urgency is very important. You must set it up from the beginning. Many salespeople have heard, "I won't ever make a snap decision." A response that works for many is, "I agree with you, Mr. Prospect, you shouldn't make a snap decision. However, sometimes you may need to make an efficient decision. Here's what I mean by 'efficient decision': Let's say that in the corner of the kitchen you see what appears to be a black line of dirt on the baseboard. During a closer look, you touch the wall and it literally crumbles at the touch. *Termites,* you think. So you call the exterminator and ask them to come out immediately to investigate. You take fast action to rid your house of the pests that could hurt your investment. You didn't make a snap decision, you made an *efficient* one."

You need to go into detail so the prospect feels the emotion of the moment. As I said previously, most people buy on emotion rather than logic, so it is very important that emotions constantly play a part in your presentation.

Point Five: Ask for the Order

How many times do we give a fantastic presentation with all the bells and whistles, emotion, facts, and persuasive points; we overcome objections; we create a sense of urgency; and we even have excellent selling points; but we walk away empty-handed? This is where the fifth point comes in. Sometimes you may not have to use the fifth point; you may make the sale right after the second point or even the first point. It would be unwise to rely on that, though—you really have to master the fifth point.

The fifth point is both the most obvious and the hardest for most salespeople. This is where we generally insert our insecurities and fears of rejection. The point I am making is this: you *have* to ask for the order. None of us want to hear no. We haven't gotten the sale yet and we've tried almost everything we know to do, with one huge exception—we haven't asked the prospect for the order.

"Mr. and Mrs. Prospect, go get your checkbook and let's get this started." Or, "What is your social security number?" Or, "I need the full names of your beneficiaries."

This fifth point needs to be done without hesitation. You need to have this down. If you hesitate, your voice cracks, or you have any doubt about asking them, you will blow the sale. This is the moment of truth—the make-it-or-break-it time. Your prospect/soon-to-be client wants to buy. They gave you an appointment. They are listening to you; you have gone through your warm-up and presentation; you have even overcome their objection and given great selling points. They are waiting for you to make the decision for them—so make it and ask for the order!

If this approach is just too direct for you, try another. "Mr. Prospect, would you like to start out with $25,000 in the annuity or would $50,000 be better?" Or, "Would you like this to be bank-drafted monthly or would you prefer the discount for annual payment?" There are dozens of alternative closes, and no matter what answer they give you, it is a sale!

Another effective close is the assumptive close. This is when you simply start writing. In the insurance business we always take an application. Often I would just look down after the fourth point and start writing. Regardless of what you are selling, once you start writing the order, don't look up. Just keep writing and asking questions. "OK, Mr. Prospect what is your middle initial?" Once they give it to you, your sale has been made!

One of the best things we do as salespeople is talk, and we generally love to hear our own voices. One of the worst things we do as salespeople is talk too much. Once you make a close—no matter if it is the assumptive, direct, or alternative—be silent after you say the sentence. This is difficult, but you must master it. It may feel like the air in the room is heavy, but in all likelihood, the prospect is simply digesting your close. Be confident and keep quiet—don't snatch defeat from the jaws of victory.

What happens when, after you close, you get another objection or the same one as before? It's easy. You just restart the Five-Point Close from the beginning. There you are: You've done the warm–up, the presentation, and the Five-Point Close. On the fifth point you used the alternative close and they came back and said, "Well, Michael, we really need to talk to our daughter before we move forward." You respond, "Absolutely, I agree with you." The beautiful thing about the Five-Point Close is that you can do it again and again and never make the prospect mad. Why? Because you are agreeing with them and they get to be right. Experience shows that you should be willing to go through the Five-Point Close up to five times. If the prospect has the need and has the money, you will make the sale!

When to Cut Bait

You will not sell everyone. If we had a 100 percent closing rate we could forget the commissions, and salespeople would be paid a nice salary with a company car and expense account.

If you do follow the Five-Point Close technique, you will sell significantly more than without it. The technique applies to life situations equally as well. Agree with the objection, own it, overcome it—it's that simple. Remember, don't be defensive or let the ego get involved. If you do, more times than not you will win the battle but lose the war.

four

Active Listening

In my estimation, the majority of people talk 90 percent of the time and listen only 10 percent. The truth of the matter is that you must *listen* 90 percent of the time. If you're with a prospect and you are doing all of the talking, you will have a huge problem with making the sale.

In late 2010 my company was testing out a new marketing approach for the dental industry. The first thing we did was see if we could get anyone to sit down with us and hear our presentation. Lo and behold, we got one—quickly, too! That was a good sign. However, the agreement to hear our presentation came so quickly—way more so than we thought it would—that we didn't have any sales material ready. So we did what most good sales teams do in these situations: wing it.

I started the presentation and didn't stop talking for more than twenty minutes. My prospects never asked me anything! How could they? I was too busy speaking so fast that I sounded like an auctioneer who just had a double shot of espresso with an energy drink chaser. The point is, you must ask questions and wait patiently for their answers, and you must be a great listener. I was not prepared, and I have found that the "just wing it" strategy will almost always get you into trouble.

So how does one go about being an "active listener"? It's easy; you already know how, you just need to be reminded. Do you remember when you went on your first date with your wife? Your husband? Your first major crush? When you were with that person driving in the car, at the restaurant, or walking into the movie, you were so very attentive to their every need. You were opening the car door, saying thank you and you're welcome, looking them in the eye, and asking them if you could get them something or if they were too cold.

This is the way you should attend to your prospect, patient, or client. Let them know you care just by being silent enough to observe their needs. Some basics to remember:

1. Look into their right eye (from your point of view). This is easier for you, and when you concentrate on one point, you appear to be *very* focused. Moreover, you cannot physically look into both eyes at the same time, so this strategy helps to keep your eyes from darting back and forth, which makes it appear as though you're not sincerely interested in what the prospect is saying.

2. Lean slightly forward in your chair. This shows that you're very interested in their opinion. It also helps you stay focused on them and avoid being distracted by the surroundings.

3. After your client makes a comment or asks a question, it is very important to acknowledge it.

First say, "That's a great question/observation." Or, "Yes, I believe I understand. To be certain, what I hear you saying is . . ." This will give your client a level of comfort—a certainty that you are paying attention and that you are communicating.

So to make this really easy: sit up, look them in the right eye, lean forward, and repeat what you heard them say. That is active listener 101.

If you listen, your prospect, client, or partner will tell you how to close the deal. During the building of rapport and the warm-up phase, the clues will come forth—write them down. Then, when needed, do the Colombo: while rubbing your forehead, say, "OK, just to make sure I got this, you said that if you ever get out of this house, you want to build a new home with a tennis court? Did I get that right, Mary? Is that what you said?"

Your prospects want to buy from you, they truly do, but they don't want to come out and say it. They want you to say it for them. If you listen carefully enough they will tell you *exactly* how to close them. Practice active listening with everyone, your wife, husband, children, coworkers—even your boss.

five

_____ __ __ __ _____

Building Rapport

Most of us like to do business with people to whom we have some kind of connection. This of course is not always the case. For example, if you going into a mall to buy a pair of tennis shoes, it probably makes no difference to you that the person fetching your size 11 Nikes has a lot in common with you. However, you do want to at least establish some basic rapport with the individual, an understanding that you're the customer and are in need of new shoes and they are the shoe expert and can help you with your purchase. This is very easily done because the obvious is taking place. You're in a shoe store and you ask an employee a specific question.

When you are selling something a little less tangible or perhaps more complex, such as an insurance policy, a medical procedure, a lifestyle, or an investment, you must find common ground beyond the obvious. So many professionals in fields such as law, accounting, and medicine miss this and rely strictly on their credentials to sell themselves. Of course, if the situation is dire, this works fine. But if not—if you're simply looking for a new law firm to handle your company's legal matters—it's an entirely different situation.

A quick way to begin the process is to think visually. Make a quick assessment of the room, observing things such clothing, jewelry, automobiles, art, and photos—anything that may give you a clue to the individual's likes and dislikes. Once you do this, find something that you have in common, something that you truly find interesting and are knowledgeable about; at an appropriate time during the meeting, make a comment about this discovery. You must be sincere in this find; do *not* fake it!

So what happens if there is nothing visual that you can use to forge a connection? Then you must start by asking questions—not like an investigator in an interrogation, but with simple, easy questions that may lead to the discovery of some commonalities: Where are your children attending school? Are you a member of any clubs? What is your favorite place for lunch? Do you have any travel plans coming up soon? Remember, people like to do business with people like themselves. Find the commonalities.

If you are successful, that's great! Build on the connection you've just established, but be careful not to over do it. Everyone has been in a situation in which someone is trying way too hard to be your friend. It makes you uncomfortable and it's embarrassing to everyone involved—including the pursuer. Once you have organically established a good rapport, you can move on to developing a business relationship. This may take several encounters. Sometimes if it's a small purchase or investment it can happen on the first encounter. I have even experienced very large purchases on the first call after I have established a positive rapport.

There have been occasions when I have heard sales-people say that they are not interested in establishing rapport with anyone. "Either they want my services or they don't!" they say. If you have something that is so unique and rare that they must come to you and only you to get it, then OK, you don't have worry about rapport. Instead you may worry about your reputation. No one really wants to be *that* guy. So establish rapport; don't fake it, be sincere, and be yourself.

six

___ __ __ __ ___

Pacing and Mirroring

Pacing

It is very important to allow your prospect to set the pace of the presentation. If you attempt to control this, you may make the sale, but the client could soon get the dreaded buyer's remorse and cancel the transaction. You have probably heard of the "pace car" in car racing. This is the car that drives ahead of the other cars in formation to set the speed for the start of the race. It usually takes a few laps to establish the pace; once it does so, the pace car will exit the track and the race is on.

In your presentation or meeting it is the same way. You must follow the lead of the pace car, which in this case is your client, prospect, or patient. Sometimes the prospect will want to rush the pace and you will be tempted to hurry or even immediately jump to the bottom line. Such actions are usually a clear attempt by the prospect to hijack the whole presentation. If this occurs, you either have to stop the presentation and reschedule for a time that allows the prospect to slow down and listen to your valuable information, or do as they requested and cut to the chase. This is a gut call. I wish I could just say one size fits all, but it doesn't.

For instance, you'll need to have a response if you are in the middle of the warm-up and your client interrupts you mid-sentence and says something like this: "Michael, I am very busy and I don't have much time. Please tell me the highlights of this policy and I will think about it and get back to you."

When confronted with a statement such as this, I frequently respond as follows: "I apologize, Bill, I was under the impression that this was very important to you and your family. This is very crucial to your business, and I would rather not glide over it lightly. Let's reschedule this for a time when you can afford to give it the attention it deserves."

When I use this, it usually jolts them into giving me more time and not rushing me, or they will say, "Call me to reschedule." On occasion, they will blow me off when I try to reschedule; either way, I do not want to waste their time or mine. This approach sends a clear signal that you're not just trying to make a fast sale, but that you are authentic in your presentation.

Most times, however, after the rapport and warm-up are established, you can begin to pace the presentation as well as when to close. If the prospect says, "Michael, I like it, let's buy this one," it is a clear sign to shut up and button up the sale with paperwork, payment, signatures, or whatever the case may be. Do not keep selling! The prospects just changed the pace in a positive manner. Ensure that they are clear on exactly what they are buying and begin setting up the order.

Pacing is a natural thing if you use your God-given ability of deductive reasoning. You have been doing it most of your life with your relationships. Your friends probably often say, "Hey man, you need pace yourself and slow down." Generally this means you are moving faster than the rest of the group and you're way out of sync. Look around and measure the pace of the conversation. For example, how many questions are you getting? If there are any, how quickly are they coming? These observations will tell you if you need to speed up or slow down. If you don't know and the prospect is not giving you any signs, it's always better to go slowly. The pace will come. Let your prospect set it; eventually they will exit the track, and you can then be the pace car.

Mirroring

Again, this is something you have been doing all your life. For instance, consider the times when you have been with a good friend and their phone rang. Chances are that when your friend answered and began a conversation with someone, you knew fairly soon who was on the other end just by the way your friend was talking. Your friend was mirroring the caller's words and tone because we tend to mirror the people we admire.

When you are giving a sales presentation you should mirror your client. If your client sits up and is leaning forward in his chair, you should, too. If you're at dinner and your client orders a cappuccino and is relaxing after the meal, you should do the same. These small actions allow your prospect to get comfortable with you. However, it is important to remember not to be phony. If your customer orders a double shot of espresso and you don't like espresso, don't get the same thing. Order coffee or a coke, whatever is appropriate for you.

Early in my sales career, I was working in rural Indiana and I had a sales appointment with a farmer and his wife. The appointment was set for five o'clock in the morning; it was harvest time, so early in the morning was the only time they could see me. I arrived at 4:45 a.m., and the wife greeted me at the door. The first thing that hit me was the wonderful aroma of bacon and pancakes. She escorted me to the kitchen, where her husband was just finishing up his breakfast. I won't lie, I was in my mid-twenties, so I could eat with the best of them, and that morning I had eaten only an apple on the way over from the hotel. I easily could have had a pound of crispy bacon and a half dozen pancakes, especially from the farm griddle I was staring at. But I knew that I needed to get to the presentation before the farmer got out to the field. I was offered breakfast but I politely declined, asking only for coffee. You don't want to be insulting, but you have a job to do, and if time is of the essence, don't waste it!

Remember that your prospect will send you several signals in the first few minutes of your meeting. Your job is to build an honest rapport, find the pace of the meeting, and mirror your prospects to help put them at ease. This should all become fairly easy to you once you practice it a few times.

Part 2
Homework

———————— ————————

L ist the parts of the Five-Point Close:

1. _____

2. _____

3. _____

4. _____

5. _____

The characteristics of an active listener are:

1. Maintain _____ _____ at all times.

2. Focus on the _____ _____ in particular.

3. When it comes to posture, remember to lean _____.

4. As soon as your prospect asks a question, you need to immediately _____ by _____ the question.

5. During the presentation be sure to take plenty of _____.

The cornerstones of building rapport are:

1. Find _____ ground with your customer.

2. Quickly assess the prospect's environment to _____ more about them.

3. Use what you've learned to pose a number of appropriate _____.

4. Most importantly, be _____ and be _____.

The fundamental elements of pacing and mirroring are:

1. It is very important to allow your prospect to set the _____ of the conversation.

2. The one crucial aspect of the presentation is that the salesperson remains in _____.

3. Be sure to _____ the prospect's body language during the presentation.

4. Your prospect will send you many _____ in the first few minutes of your meeting. Be sure to pay attention.

5. Once the prospect is ready to buy, you need to stop _____.

Part 3

Take It from Me: Life Lessons

life lessons

——— — — — — ———

This book would not be complete without my addressing the catalyst that led me to write the book—a pivotal time in my life. The story begins with the death and birth of a salesman. The date was February 19, 1992, and my wife, Stacye, and I had gone out to dinner and asked my mother to stay with our two young daughters. During dinner we were going over some of the events of the previous week. I had a lot of insecurities about following in the shadow of my father-in-law, and I was bothered because I felt that I was not getting any credit for what I was doing (actually, I was being selfish and self-centered). We were discussing this and I believe my wife said to me, wisely, "You'll get the credit you deserve."

To bring this into context it is important to know the reason that I felt that way. Jack, my father-in-law and mentor, and I had launched a new company about six months prior and had been working very hard. The reason I was disappointed was because we were putting a lot of our own cash into the business. Jack was guiding and coaching me through the process of starting a new venture. In truth, he was an entrepreneur, a leader, and a marketing genius. He was very charismatic, and I was lucky to be taught by the best. Deep down I knew all that, yet I allowed my ego to get involved, because I wanted to get some credit for financing and cocreating the company. We didn't have a lot of money at the time and we were trying to get the venture going on a shoestring. In fact, if it wasn't for American Express, we'd never have gotten it off the ground.

My wife and I had a great dinner and drove home. As I opened the door, my mother ran out waving her hands and yelling. I didn't know what to think! She said, "Jack has had a heart attack and they can't get a pulse!" He was at a nearby hospital in Plano (just north of Dallas). We immediately jumped back into the car, I turned on the emergency blinkers, and we sped down the highway as fast as I could go, breaking all laws on the way.

When we arrived at the hospital, I jumped out of the car and sprinted inside, not really knowing what was happening. Frantic, I was yelling and looking for Jack. I looked in each exam room in the emergency room, but there was hardly anybody around. I kept yelling, "Where is Jack? Where is Jack?" Finally I came to a room, pulled back the curtain, and there he was. It didn't look like him: his eyes were partially open, staring straight at the ceiling, and there was no life left in them. He had died just before arriving at the hospital. At that time a doctor came in with a nurse and told me the news. It was a surreal moment, like an out-of-body experience. I could not believe what I was seeing. I was then led to the family waiting room with my wife while we went through all of the emotions that follow such an unexpected tragedy. I expressed my shock by screaming, crying, and yelling. It was not a good moment for me. I don't regret my reaction; I just know it as the way I felt—it was perhaps the lowest moment of my life.

We left the hospital after about an hour and drove back to our house in total shock. As we turned the corner on our street, I remember thinking, *This is the worst it gets.* I felt that my friend, my mentor, and my father was somewhere on the other side, somewhere where I couldn't see him or be with him. It was a strange feeling.

My wife went to inform her brother of their father's death and I stayed home with our daughters, who were sleeping. I was up all night wondering how we were going to go forward with the business. Everything was in my name. I felt I could handle the business because I was already handling the day-to-day operations, but I didn't know what was about to take place. I had no idea that a storm had been developing and was about to come raining down on my head. I felt so many emotions, ranging from grief to fear to anxiety. I was going to be "*the man,*" and at thirty-one, my shoulders had to widen to take on the responsibility. We were young with a young family, and our business was just getting off the ground. We were working off of American Express cards, we were cash poor, and we were robbing Peter to pay Paul.

Start at the Bottom

Sixty miles north of Detroit is a small town called Flint. Chances are that people who live outside of Michigan had never heard of Flint until filmmaker Michael Moore popularized the town with his documentary *Roger and Me*. A very successful movie, *Roger and Me* accurately portrayed a downtrodden Flint after GM pulled tens of thousands of jobs from the area in the mid-1980s. That is not to say that I completely agree with the movie's portrayal of Roger Smith (then the CEO of General Motors). I believe that it was somewhat slanted; however, the point was made.

Flint, Michigan, is not the sexiest place in America by any stretch. In fact, *Forbes* has consistently placed Flint on its list of the top ten *worst* places to live. Believe it or not, though, it was not always like that. In its heyday from 1955 to 1970, Flint had its own vibe and was a pretty happening kind of place—especially for a small town. After all, General Motors was producing more cars and trucks in that city than anywhere else in the world. Great jobs, great benefits, and the great, big, powerful United Auto Workers Union were all throughout Flint, Saginaw, Detroit, and many other towns in southeastern Michigan. Unfortunately, Flint's heyday did not last once the automobile industry began experiencing a downward slide that some claim is still going on. I think the flash point came in 1973 with the infamous energy crisis, the oil embargo, and the birth of the oil cartel (OPEC).

Watching President Jimmy Carter on national TV with his cardigan sweater, asking that we all "conserve our energy and turn our thermostats to sixty-eight degrees," is a sticking point in the memories of many. I was too young to understand, but it truly was the beginning of the end for the residents of Flint and Genesee County, Michigan. Oil prices shot up, gas prices spiked, and gas stations ran out of gas. The recession in the auto industry had hit fast and hard, and the entire area felt the effects.

Over 80 percent of the Tri-City area's population (those in Saginaw, Bay City, and Midland) depended on the auto industry for their livelihoods, and a strong case could be made that upwards of 95 percent of the population were influenced dramatically by the ups and downs of the auto industry. My parents and our extended family were tied to the industry, as well.

My mother was the second-oldest of seven children. Her strong character came from her Irish father and French-Canadian mother (who incidentally fought about their ancestry on a regular basis, or so I am told). The challenges that she overcame—an alcoholic father and a mother who worked outside the home, contrary to the norm at the time—ensured that she developed a strong sense of perseverance. My mother was, and I believe still is, a strong Democrat; she was very active in the local UAW; she worked for Fisher Body, a division of GM; and she insisted in 1976 that if Jimmy Carter didn't beat Gerald Ford, we would all be doomed. She was an incredibly independent woman, and I have learned much from her.

My father was one of four children. Unfortunately, for many reasons, his mother and father couldn't take care of their children. All four of them were put into an orphanage in Flint. Of course, this had a significant impact on their lives and the type of people they would become. My father joined the Marines in 1952 and fought in the Korean War. He came back in 1955, met my mother in 1958, and they got married soon after. I was born in 1960, joining my older brother from my mother's previous marriage. My parents had two more children and as 50 percent of marriages do, theirs ended in divorce. It was 1968 and I was seven years old. Though I did not know it at the time, this naturally impacted my life, especially in my early adulthood.

In 1971 my mother had another child, a daughter with her third husband. As I grew older, I watched my mother struggle to support her five children with little to no support from our father. Money was *always* tight, even though my mother had a good job at GM with good benefits. Supporting a household of six on one income was not easy. All of this really changed my perception of money forever.

Over the years, my relationships with my siblings have ebbed and flowed. However, what stands out in my mind is that we always stuck together when times were tough. In many ways, our uncles and aunts helped raise us. It was all about family back then. Though times were difficult and we did not always get along, my family has helped to make me who I am, and my experiences from birth until now have helped me become successful at what I do. From mowing the five acres that we shared with my uncle who lived behind us to taking out the trash, I have had responsibilities for as long as I can remember. There's nothing unusual about that. Growing up in an environment in which chances to earn money and make a better life were few and far between, you had to learn to make your own opportunities, come up with your own ideas, and make them work.

LIFE LESSON:
You make your own opportunities;
you make your own luck.

Seize Your Opportunities

When you grow up in a place and family where money is tight (to say the least) and you have a desire for nice things, you either have to accept that you can't have them or find a way to earn them. For me, that meant making my own opportunities and making money by doing odd jobs; in effect, that meant selling folks on services that I could do for them from a very young age.

My first experience with making my own money came one winter when I was twelve. We were getting our usual two hundred inches of snow, so I took out an ad in *The Flint Journal* for snow-shoveling. It read, "Will shovel your driveway for $7.00." I had my own "teenage" telephone in my room (a beige, touch-tone Trimline), for which I paid $8.49 per month. Customers, mostly thrifty, elderly widows, began to call, and I figured that I was going to get rich. How hard could it be? Knock out a couple of driveways after school and five on the weekends. Boom—I would make $75 to $100 a week! A fortune for a twelve-year-old in 1972.

I rode the bus, carrying my shovel (which was actually a spade), for an hour to get to my first job. The house was old and had a huge gravel and dirt semi-circular driveway. It took nearly five hours to shovel that driveway. If I hadn't been thirteen, I am convinced that I would have dropped dead of three heart attacks and a stroke. As it was, I nearly froze to death. I thought the lady would come out with some hot chocolate, a coke, or a glass of water. Instead, she would peek through her curtains every hour or so to check on me, probably shocked that I hadn't quit or frozen into a statue.

Finally I finished. It was dark by the time I walked up to her front door. The old gal opened the door, and since it had taken so much time and the driveway was *so* long, I thought she would give me a little extra over the seven-dollar rate I had quoted. No deal; she handed me seven one-dollar bills, said "thank you," and shut the door.

I learned my very first business lesson at that moment. I realized I could either feel sorry for myself or chalk the experience up as a valuable lesson. I now look back on that experience as the reason I decided to go into sales.

That spring our school had a fundraiser where we were supposed to sell—get this—lightbulbs, of all things. I was only interested because the person who sold the most would win a fifty-dollar savings bond and the runner up would get a twenty-five-dollar bond. I picked up my package of bulbs and started going door–to-door. I memorized my presentation and hit the surrounding neighborhoods. I sold boxes and boxes of lightbulbs and realized that I was pretty good at selling.

One day my mother and I went to a wholesale outlet for business owners, similar to a Sam's Club. I was intrigued, and while I was looking around, I saw a small box of lightbulbs in addition to the giant pallets of everything from pickles to soft drinks. In a flash, I thought, *This is my road to riches.* I ran over to the store clerk and asked to speak to the manager. He pointed me to a man wearing a tie. I walked right up to him and said, "Hi, my name is Michael McIntyre, and I can get you a great deal on lightbulbs!"

He started to dismiss me as any adult would when faced with such an outrageous proclamation from a kid, but then his face changed and I could see he was intrigued. "Oh yeah, how much?" he asked.

Just when I started to answer, my mother grabbed me by the arm and said, "Michael, come on, let's get going. We don't have time for that." Man, I almost had a deal!

LIFE LESSON:
You can ask anyone at anytime for the order.

I won that contest not because I sold a vast quantity of lightbulbs through a wholesaler, but because I worked hard and sold vast quantities of lightbulbs door-to-door. When they announced my name over the PA system in homeroom that morning, you would have thought I had won the Pulitzer Prize! I *loved* it. It made quite a splash and for a little while I was the center of attention. When someone asked how I did it, I said, "I just did." I was famous for a little while, I had cash in my pocket, and it sure beat shoveling snow. I was hooked on sales!

LIFE LESSON:
Enjoy your wins. You'll need that energy
to carry you through your losses.

It wasn't the money that did it; it was the recognition it brought me that made that win so special. I found what I was good at, and I liked that people recognized that talent. People who think that salespeople are only in the job for the money are often way off the mark. Recognition for a job well done is vital to the sales professional. Face it, even the best salespeople lose the sale once in a while and that's a blow to the ego. Recognition boosts self-confidence, and self-confident salespeople make more sales.

LIFE LESSON:
Sometimes the recognition will
go further than the money.

After my successful career as a lightbulb salesman, I took on a job as a paperboy. What a waste of time it seemed. You would deliver papers to people who often didn't even see you, and then you had to beg to collect their subscription fees. More often than not, you were greeted with resentment and something to the effect of: "Get with me next week, boy." When you finally did collect from everyone, you made a whopping twelve dollars for six weeks of work. It was back-breaking work at times, especially on Sundays. Growing up in a time when hard work was rewarded and salespeople were underappreciated, it took me a while to learn that you get more from your *yak* than from breaking your back.

One thing that stands out about my time at Westin Elementary was my first solo crack at being a true entrepreneur at the ripe old age of fourteen. Some of the parents and teachers were using the gym at night to play basketball, and they needed someone to sweep the gym afterward and lock it up. Since I lived next door to the school, this seemed like a perfect fit for me; being a kid who was fast becoming accustomed to making his own opportunities, I put myself forward for the job. I would go to the gym at around five o'clock in the evening, watch them finish, then sweep and clean the floor so they could use it for the cafeteria the next morning. While I was there, the men gave me money to buy soft drinks from the teachers' lounge for them. The drinks were about thirty-five cents each. Looking at the prices, I started thinking about that warehouse club where my mother bought things in bulk.

The next time she went, I went with her and priced the soft drinks, which were only *ten* cents each with the refund deposit on the bottle. Being ambitious and wanting to make money and gain recognition, it didn't take me long to start selling those cheaper soft drinks for twenty-five cents to my captive market at the gym. I began a nice little business for myself. I did have some pushback from the principal. He felt it was taking business away from the vendor who supplied the school, and he wasn't certain that I was allowed to resell the cokes from the wholesale store. I didn't realize it at the time, but the Five-Point Close was already active. My response was, "You're right, Mr. Wilson. We are taking money from the vendor, but I am not selling during school hours, it is a better bargain for you and your friends, and it helps me out." His knowledge of my home situation was more than likely a swaying factor, and I certainly used it to my advantage.

LIFE LESSON:
You have to seize the advantages that you
have or can make to be successful.

My next venture was to breed calico cats. I just *knew* those cats were going to make me rich!

Get Educated

I was pretty young when I graduated from high school, and I joined the United States Air Force fresh from the graduation podium. I thought that I could join the air force and go to school at the same time—at least that's what the recruiter said, and I believed him. I chose the air force for two reasons: One, they really touted academics in the recruiting video. Two, I thought I would look good in blue. That's it, nothing more.

When you go into the air force, you go in with all kinds of glorified thoughts of what it is going to be like. I am here to tell you, an air force recruit learns some very tough life lessons very quickly. I chose my "dream" location of Little Rock, Arkansas—mainly because I was seventeen, more than a little nervous, and thought that my recruiter would be there. My lessons started the first day I arrived, which was the Saturday before Labor Day. The only thing that got me through the first three days of basic training was my ability to adapt to any situation. That ability was put to the test as soon as I stepped off the bus at Lackland Air Force Base.

Our drill instructor was waiting for us, Smokey hat and all, and my introduction to the air force began with two hours of picking up and putting down our suitcases as a group. We did this for two hours before we figured out that we had to do it in exact unison. Welcome to the air force.

LIFE LESSON:
The air force offers a great education in teamwork and discipline. Apply this to everything that you do in life and you will succeed.

It was a long holiday weekend with only the one change of clothing. We were supposed to be issued uniforms, but that office did not open until Tuesday. We took a lot of ribbing from the other boot camp attendees who had already been in for a while. We would march by—very badly I might add—and the other troops, who had nicknamed us because of our differently colored clothes, would sing songs like, "Rainbow, rainbow, don't be blue. Our recruiter screwed us, too!" By Tuesday I couldn't wait to get my head shaved and my green uniform issued. Then they called us "pickles."

LIFE LESSON:
It's no fun being the new guy, but to get to the top and be good, you have to start at the bottom.

Take the First Step

Maybe it was foresight on my part or perhaps just luck, but after my honorable discharge from the air force in the summer of 1982, I loaded up my car and set out for Dallas—I just knew that I would be successful there. I attended night classes at the University of Texas at Dallas to finish my bachelor's degree in administration; while there I met a banker who was providing financing for an upscale men's clothing store. In early 1983 I got my first sales job—selling clothes.

One day I came back from lunch and I noticed a Rolls-Royce in the parking lot. Intrigued, I went into the store and watched my boss sell a young man in his thirties four suits and ten ties, worth somewhere in the range of $22,000 dollars. With his job clearly done for the day, my boss invited his new best customer to go next door for a drink. The customer said, "Invite the new guy, he looks like a great salesman." So I went with them. Little did I know I was about to meet my fate by being recruited into the big insurance arena. At twenty-two years old, fresh from the air force, and less than worldly, this all made quite an impression on me. There was a guy who had clearly made his way in the world. I *wanted* that level of success.

After speaking to me for a little while the customer told me, "Michael, you should be selling insurance; you can make a great deal of money and help people in the process." (He might not have said those exact words, but it was pretty close.) He got my attention, so I called him and started the process. I figured it would take a tremendous amount of studying and training to be successful in this new venture, but it really didn't. I attended a class at night to learn the various insurance laws for Texas, and then I took the test to obtain my license. It was probably thirty days from the day I called that man until I was in the car, headed for Indiana with my new sales manager, learning how to sell insurance. At the time, I didn't really understand why we were going to Indiana, but now I do—that was where the "good leads" were, where deals were being closed. It was a good training ground. I watched my sales manager make several presentations in people's houses over the course of four days. I watched how he masterfully handled each objection and the timing of his rebuttals. While in between appointments my sales manager would go over all of the benefits of the contract with me and quiz me on the finer details. From the very first presentation he made, I thought, *Hey, I can do this, and I can do it better!* I just *felt* it. I went back to Texas, picked up my insurance license, and was ready to go!

I had a license to sell insurance, but no reliable transportation, and the hot leads were four hundred miles away from Dallas in a town called Wink. I had a 1970 Monte Carlo, and I ran out of gas no less than ten times times. It got terrible mileage (about forty feet to the gallon) and I didn't feel good about driving it very far, so I called my uncle and asked him if he would rent a car for me to drive. He did so, and I was on my way to Wink, Texas. I had no idea how far it was and I didn't care. After driving for about six hours, I started to figure it out.

I eventually checked into a hotel room, practiced my presentation, and crawled into bed. The next day I went to my first appointments. I made four presentations in two days, but I really didn't know what I was doing and didn't make a single sale. I knew the product basics, but didn't quite understand the art of selling. My enthusiasm and work ethic had carried me to that point, but I needed to figure out how to make the sale.

After two days of no sales I started to worry. I had $700 left to my name, the hotel was $35 a night, and I knew that the rental was going to cost a couple hundred dollars. Finally, during the last call on the third day, I hit pay dirt! I made a sale that netted me more than $1,000. While I knew it would happen, I also couldn't believe it! I made three more sales that week before I drove back to Dallas on cloud nine. It was the shortest eight-hour drive ever.

I was very excited on Monday when I turned in my sales. The woman in the accounting department told me to come back after lunch to pick up my check. I thought, *What kind of check?* I knew that my commission was a certain percentage of the premiums that I had collected, but I had no idea how much. I went to lunch in the brand-new Galleria Mall where our offices were located. When I came back, I walked into the office and a nice-looking lady of about forty said in a Texas drawl, "Hey, honey, you did good your first week out of the chute. We couldn't verify funds on two of your sales, but I don't think you'll starve, sugar."

She handed me the check, I thanked her, put it in my coat pocket, and headed for the elevators. I wanted to look at it, but I thought I should wait until I got to my car to evaluate my fortune or lack thereof. When I got to my car, I excitedly pulled out the envelope, opened it, and did a double take at the numbers. The check was made out to me in the amount of $4,800.96—that's four thousand eight hundred dollars and ninety-six cents! My heart skipped a beat. At the bottom of the statement it said, "Total Earned for the Week: $6,400."

Now, you have to put all this into context. My previous W-2, which was for my last year in the air force, showed earnings of $5,400. That was for the *year*. And in just one *week* I had made more than in the previous earning year. I was hooked! I knew I had found my calling.

The next thing I did was look to see what bank the check was drawn on. It was the same bank at the Galleria—how cool was that? I went into the bank, cashed my check, put all forty-eight of those one hundred–dollar bills in my front pocket, and walked to my car like I owned Texas. It was *great*.

LIFE LESSON:
Belief in yourself won't get you everywhere,
but it will get you a very long way.

Move Past Disappointments

Before receiving my honorable discharge, I had spent four years as a security specialist in Little Rock, Arkansas, with the strategic air command. Prior to that, I watched the deterioration of the economy in my homeland, the great state of Michigan, which was the catalyst for my leaving as quickly as I could after high school graduation. While in the air force I received my associate's degree from Arkansas State University.

In 1979 my uncle Mark had moved to Dallas, Texas, and I'd visited him there several times while I was in the service. Once I was discharged I packed my bags and immediately moved to Dallas—happiness was Little Rock AFB in my rearview mirror. I arrived in Dallas and began working at Lone Star Cadillac, driving cars for six dollars an hour. What happened from there was interesting.

As I've mentioned, I worked at a few different places before I finally got into the insurance business. In 1983 I passed the insurance exam and was recruited into a company that sold life insurance, which is where I met my wife, Stacye. In 1984 I left that company for a better opportunity selling health insurance to self-employed small business owners. Things went pretty well for quite a while. I was out there learning the health insurance business and doing really well. I realized that you can do even better when you have people working for you, which I did. In June of 1985 Stacye and I were married. My brother, who had just moved to Dallas to sell health insurance with me, served as the best man. Things were going great; I was married and working with my brother. We did very well for the next several years, growing an agency and perfecting our craft.

Then in 1991 it all changed. The country began looking for a national health coverage plan, promoted by President Bill Clinton. The company I was representing changed directions and I found myself essentially out of a job. At that time, Stacye's father, Jack, was a retired insurance entrepreneur who was looking to get back into the business, so we got together and started an agency doing estate planning. It was good timing. My wife and I didn't have a lot, but we had built up to having $20,000 in the bank and things were going OK, so we had a few dollars to make this thing work. Even though we didn't have a lot of cash, we had credit cards that were working and valuable. So Jack and I came up with a plan. We took a small office I already had and expanded it. It was a really good feeling for me; Jack gave me the necessary confidence that I had not yet found. He let me do what I knew was right; I suppose it was validation in a way.

In August 1991 we started our own business. It was extremely challenging because we really didn't know what we were doing, but we knew how to recruit, train, and motivate. We spent enormous amounts of time and money developing the business. On the home front, with two young children, long or sleepless nights were not uncommon. I'd be out at the call center in Denton, Texas, thirty miles from home, at 7:00 a.m. and work until 11:00 p.m., then drive home and do the whole thing over again. It wasn't an easy time but it wasn't a bad time, either.

I'll never forget our first sale: I was so excited—talk about a paradigm shift! Everything looked quite different. I woke up the next morning, and on the way to work it was like somebody had given me a brand-new pair of glasses. We had actually given birth to this new venture, and making that *one sale* after putting in tens of thousands of dollars and work hours was validation of our belief that we were doing the right thing. With that one sale we knew it would work.

We weren't making money but we were starting to bring revenue into the company. The economy was doing poorly at best. There were a lot of people looking for work, so we had no problem recruiting talented people. Our biggest problem was that we were completely undercapitalized. We were operating completely on American Express cards and whatever cash we had coming in. We put a hodgepodge staff together and started training them to go out and sell the product. Jack and I shared a little office with a conference table, at which we sat across from each other. Sitting across from him day in and day out, I learned much that I have been able to apply to my career. He was an absolute master with people. Though Jack sometimes had a hard time talking about things and he could get temperamental—as could I—I knew I was being taught by a consummate professional, and that was very special for me. So in spite of his pushing my buttons and his tendency to jump on me for every small mistake, I knew the relationship was perfect. I accepted it despite the occasional hurt feelings and bruised ego because I knew that he wanted what was best for us.

All of this changed when he died on February 19, 1992. Within two weeks of the funeral I received a call from someone at a national newspaper, saying that they had interviewed one of our salespeople, were going to press in two weeks, and wanted to know if we wanted to comment.

Apparently the newspaper had conducted a "sting" operation and secretly taped one of our representatives when giving their presentation. Unfortunately, that rep made misleading comments and answered questions that should have been referred to a lawyer.

I immediately called our attorneys and we did some checking. It was not a favorable article. The following two weeks were crazy. We were on CSPAN; *Newsweek* and the Associated Press were calling for interviews; lawsuits were being filed against the organization alleging misrepresentation and the unauthorized practice of law. The lawsuits were politically motivated; our company had made several powerful enemies. When forging a whole new industry, there is a lot of blood spilled in the early days of battle.

We were in crisis mode. My attorney helped me get in touch with the former attorney general in Maine, David, with whom I spoke briefly because there was going to be a suit filed in the state of Maine. I remember talking to him on the phone and he said, "Yes, Michael, if you listen to the television in the background, the attorney general and the governor are getting ready to hold a press conference. You can hear it as they start talking about your organization."

I hired him, sent him a check for a retainer, and he flew down to Dallas on Easter Sunday. I picked David up at the airport and took him to his hotel so he could coach me on how to deal with these crisis situations. The next day he came to the office and we started damage control. The first thing he did was advise us and our attorney to go to Oklahoma, where our vendor's headquarters were located. So we chartered a small plane, flew to Oklahoma, and had a meeting with them. After our meeting, which lasted about an hour, we were walking to lunch on the small town's main street when David pulled me aside and said, "Michael, you need a friend; your vendor and their attorneys are *not* your friends!"

Upon returning to Dallas, David made a few phone calls, one of which resulted in an appointment the next morning with one of the biggest law firms in the city. He then explained to me that there had been a huge conflict of interest by the law firm that represented both our company and our vendors. It was a major business blunder and I had to try to correct it—my hope was that it wasn't too late. I really was missing Jack; I desperately wanted to know what he thought. Thankfully, David made me feel as though I finally had someone giving me good, truthful advice.

Going to bed that night I felt that the next day we would start to fix that misunderstood mess. Little did I know what was coming next. We went to downtown Dallas the next day, met with our new counsel, retained them, and began to try to turn the situation around.

Over the course of the next few days, we had several meetings. During that time I was introduced to a young attorney named Jeff. He was a little younger than me but very smart and likeable. He called me a week later and explained that he had arranged a meeting with the firm's senior partner for the following day. The next day I got there and was shown to the big conference room on the top floor of the building. My attorney and the senior partner came in, and the senior partner did all the talking about all the different problems we had. Then he finally got to the meat of the conversation and said, "Michael, what you need to do is file bankruptcy."

I thought, *Oh God!* It hit me like a ton of bricks. There I was, thirty-one years old. I knew that I owed some money, and I had major lawsuits coming in left and right, as well as some serious business concerns to deal with, but I couldn't help but think, *How can we sit here and file bankruptcy, not pay the vendors, not pay my agents, and still have integrity?* I knew even then that this is a small town, a small world, and if we wanted to survive, if we wanted to make it happen, bankruptcy wasn't the right thing for us to do.

I took a hard look at the options that were available. By that time my wife and I had roughly $200,000 saved and owed about $250,000 on our home. I'd been told to pay off our house, so we put $100,000 towards our house and used the rest of the money to try and get out of the mess we were in.

Over the next several weeks it just got worse. Not only was the loss of Jack still fresh, but I found myself bursting into tears just driving down the street. I was in panic most of the time. While I did exercise and run a lot, which helped me keep my sanity, I truly felt as if I was on my own, because I had not yet accepted Jesus Christ. Even worse, I didn't know how to pray for help.

In the end, I stuck to my convictions and chose not to file bankruptcy. Instead, Jeff and I fought and settled, one by one, every claim brought against the company. It took over eight months and all of the money I had left, but we did it. Ultimately we stopped selling and closed the company. It was very strange to go from being part of a very exciting, fast-growing company, working side-by-side with my father-in-law, to Jack being dead, the company being closed, and spending months fighting legal battles. It was a very bleak time.

LIFE LESSON:
If something threatens your business,
be aggressive. Fight back. Get the right
players on your team! Pray, listen,
and take appropriate action.

Maximize Your Strengths

Being penny-wise and dollar-foolish can spell failure for sales professionals. If you need help, get it. If you think *maybe* you could use some help, get it. If you think you can do it all yourself, you might be able to, but at what cost? The key is to leverage your talent to its fullest potential. That means hiring other people to do the mundane tasks so that you can use your time more profitably. A successful salesperson realizes early in their career how to accentuate their positives attributes.

Early in my career, when I was selling health insurance, I used leads the company provided. Every Monday we would go to the home office, turn in our sales, and collect a check and a new deck of leads. I would then go home, get on the phone, and set up my appointments for the next day. As leads usually go, some were great and some weren't.

After making as many appointments as I could, I would travel and "run my appointments." During the day, I stopped at any pay phone I could find to set appointments for the next day. This was before cell phones and the Internet. It wasn't easy—and when the weather was bad it was really hard. However, in those days that was what worked; as long as you had the self-confidence to deal with plenty of rejection, you had a good chance of succeeding.

This was in late 1986 and I had been married for about a year and a half. My wife sometimes traveled with me, especially if I went somewhere interesting like Gulfport, Mississippi, or Corpus Christi, Texas. One rainy day we were in Galveston, Texas, and my wife suggested that she set my appointments for the next day. It would free up my time so we could go to dinner and a movie that night.

My reaction was, "Are you sure you can do this? You haven't ever sold anything."

She replied, "I have been listening to you for the past year and a half. I know the script by heart!"

So I gave her the leads, told her what I needed for the next day, and left to run my appointments. Two things happened: One, I found that I was able to be totally focused on making sales and not on setting up the next day. Two, I made *more* sales and was in a much better mood because I wasn't dealing with the hassles of scheduling and rejection.

When I got back to our hotel, Stacye had set four appointments for the next day, and I realized that dividing and conquering and focusing on my particular strength was the best way to move forward. It was the beginning of a very cool partnership. My sales doubled, my wife enjoyed it, and we had more time and money. It couldn't have been any better.

After about six weeks of this, my brother, Matt, noticed how well I was doing and wanted to know if my wife would set his appointments as well. I asked her and she agreed. It was great for her: he had the same kind of leads I did, and since he and I often traveled together, she could combine the leads to make optimal use of them.

This went well for about three months, but like most good salespeople, I got to be a prima donna pretty quickly and started believing my own press. In the health insurance business it was important that you sold to healthy people; if someone had a preexisting condition such as high blood pressure or diabetes, chances were that you could not get them a policy, especially if their current policy covered their particular condition. Most of the time, we would screen out people with preexisting conditions. There was one week in particular that was extremely challenging, and the lack of sales was beginning to get to me. After three appointments that felt like a complete waste of my time, I called my wife, forgot who I was speaking to, and made a big mistake. The conversation went something like this:

Me: Stacye?

Stacye: Oh, hi, honey, how is your day?

Me: Not worth a *bleep*!

Stacye: What is it? What's the matter?

Me: These appointments you're setting aren't worth a *bleep*! Why did you set them anyway? You know we can't sell them if they had bypass surgery last year!

Stacye: Hey, listen, Michael, don't you yell at me! I am doing this for *you*! I am working as hard as I can for us. The leads are difficult this week! In fact, *why don't you just set your own appointments from now on!*

In an instant it all flashed before my eyes: this is my wife, my confidant, the future mother of my children. She was not on the payroll or the clock. I blew it. The bell had rung and I couldn't un-ring it. I groveled and made a strong attempt to back up, but it was too late. I remember calling Stacye that evening, apologizing again, and asking her what I should say to Matt about his appointments.

She had thought that through: "I'm going to keep setting his appointments," she said. "*He* never complains. Besides, he pays me every week."

Ouch! I realized I needed that help. That help allowed me to be more successful. I took out an ad in the paper for an appointment-setter and found one: Babbette. She was a trip. She cost me five hundred dollars per week and taught me a valuable lesson: *never* complain to the people helping you.

I also learned that my value wasn't in setting appointments, because I could teach someone to do that for $500 a week while I made $4,000 in that same week doing what I was best at: selling. It just made sense.

Eventually Babbette did all my paperwork and assisted me in running the small agency that developed from that venture. We also went on to create a call center to do nothing but set agents' appointments. Salespeople like to be treated like rock stars. Set the stage and they will walk in and perform—and their performance is much better if they don't have to manage the details. For the managers out there, having the administrative and support networks in place is a good way to attract great talent and build your sales force. Treat the home office staff with respect and kindness, no matter what. Whether you have your own company or just have one assistant within a much larger company, you will have to deal with support staff.

By 1987 I had worked my way up in a national health insurance agency to become the sales manager over Texas, Louisiana, and Mississippi, and my father-in-law was kind enough to coach me on how to recruit new sales representatives. I had placed a large ad in *The Dallas Morning News*. We had an excellent turnout with more than forty salespeople showing up at the Marriott Hotel in response to the ad. In all, I invested about $2,500 in that recruiting seminar. However, the insurance company I was working with didn't get the much-needed supplies to the hotel in time, so there I was with a room full of excellent recruits and I had to go on without rate sheets or any other literature about the product or the company. In fact, I didn't even have the applications I needed to sign them up. I gave the best presentation I could and then told them all that I would get back to them.

When I had finished answering all of their questions, I walked out to the hallway and my father-in-law gave me a *lot* of coaching: "How in the hell could you not get the supplies here? You have to be ready for this! You have over forty reps that are walking out the damn door! You dropped the ball!"

I was pretty upset, so I walked over to the pay phone, called the home office, and chewed out the girl in the supply department for not getting me what I needed. Jack heard every word.

After I hung up, he looked me dead in the eye, lowered his voice, and said, "You never, ever talk to those people like that; they will make or break your career. They will lie awake at night thinking of how to screw with your deal. Pick up the phone, call the florist, and send that girl a dozen long-stemmed roses with an apology." I did, and I also called her back with a heartfelt apology.

That moment taught me to take care of the people who take care of you—especially the ones who are not on your payroll, like my wife! You must have a support network and you must appreciate those people. If they don't know that you support and appreciate them, you will not get their best efforts and you will not succeed. It goes back to one of the most basic tenets of Christianity: treat others as you would want to be treated. Would you help someone who treated you like something they stepped in?

LIFE LESSON:
You can't succeed on your own.
Figure out your strengths and hire others to do the rest. Be sure to recognize and thank the people behind the scenes.

Win the Mental Game

When your career is centered on working with other people and selling them something—be it a product, a service, or something else—the key to your success will be having your head on straight. If you seem confused, concerned, uncertain, or panicked, the chance that your customer will buy from you is fairly close to zero. In this chapter we will explore four ways that emotions can either make or break you as a salesperson. Keeping your emotions in check is vital to your success. If you can't keep them in check at least externally, find out how to do so or find another career.

We have all heard the phrase "never let them see you sweat." In other words, don't get rattled, don't panic. That is not to say that it is easy to keep your cool when faced with unfamiliar situations, difficult customers, or the outright unknown. It is in fact easier said than done, especially when dealing with change or any situation that you might not be accustomed to or comfortable with. Your emotions will always work overtime when confronted with an unfamiliar situation. If you allow them to, your emotions will begin to override your common sense. Instead of dealing with each situation factually, your brain will begin imagining the worst possible scenario and you will react to that image instead of processing the facts of the situation and acting accordingly.

In late October 2000 my company had been working on a significant deal to purchase another insurance agency that was owned by my brother and was very similar to our current business. A lot of hard work had gone into the deal, and the attorneys were finalizing the last of the contracts and other necessary paperwork.

Due to the sensitive nature of the merger, it had been kept highly confidential until the week before the papers were to be signed. In preparation for the announcement, both my brother and I had called meetings with our staff in order to individually explain the merger to them. We both believed that it was better for us to tell them in person rather than have them hear something through the office grapevine. In essence, we did not want our employees to panic. Timing is everything. After we met with the staffs from our individual companies, we planned to meet with the new, combined company and share our enthusiasm for the new venture with our staff. "Together we are stronger" was our motto, and we were excited to share it with everyone.

A special day deserves special treatment, so I decided to drive my wife's new car, a Rolls-Royce, to the meetings. I planned to take my brother out for lunch to celebrate in style, and what better way to do so than in that stunning automobile? The announcements went very well and we left to go address our combined staff, only to be met in the lobby by the COO and the attorney. Both of them had a distinctly unhappy and uncomfortable look on their faces—in essence it was "The Look." If you know anything, you know "The Look" is always the harbinger of unpleasant news. Both of the men announced a need "to talk." Given that I had recently wired a rather large sum of money and we'd spent significant funds on the day's festivities, the attorney announcing a need to talk was not what anyone wanted to hear.

Panic began to set in; my heart began to pound and my palms began to sweat. *This is not the time for the deal to fall apart!* I thought. With all of the people milling around the lobby wanting to congratulate us, I forced myself to remain calm on the outside as Jeff, my attorney, asked me if I had heard the news.

Me: Heard *what?* (Not quite in a panic, but close.)

Jeff: Tina took your car to the car wash to have it cleaned for your celebration and she ran into the building. No one is hurt, but the car is in bad shape.

In comparison with the deal falling through, that seemed minor. In those few seconds between seeing them and hearing what the "problem" was, my emotions had taken over and I had thought the worst rather than waiting for the facts. As salespeople we take our cues from people's body language, and we have to remember that we are not always right; we should await the facts before we panic. In this instance, I didn't truly panic or let them see me sweat, even though internally I had aged about five years in five minutes.

LIFE LESSON:
Don't panic on the outside—control it if you can.
The situation is seldom as bad as your
emotions lead you to believe.

Not only should you "never let them see you sweat," you should never let them see you get frustrated. In any sales career you will see many things and encounter many people, and from each of these experiences you will learn something, whether it is a skill or a tactic that will help you in your career or something that you learn not to do because it would be a detriment to your career. Either way, it is important to take these lessons to heart and use them to their fullest advantage in your career.

After a relatively successful period in life insurance and health insurance, it was time to move on to self-employed prospects. In moving to a new company, one usually does not start at the top, and there tends to be a steep learning curve in order to become accustomed to the product or service. That was the situation for me in 1986. A sales friend of mine told me about a new opportunity and after checking it out, I thought that I had found the next step in my climb up the ladder of success.

I studied the material, figured out how to make a quote, took my leads and presentation book, and set out to make my mark on this new venture. After a short period of time and having made no sales, I asked to ride along with a friend who was a great "closer" to see how he was getting the job done. He had a larger-than-life personality and made great presentations that allowed him to close the deal more often than not.

During one of my calls with him, we were sitting at a prospect's kitchen table while my friend made his presentation. He reached a point where he was getting very frustrated and wasn't closing the sale. He took his pen and tossed it straight up in the air. We all looked at it as it flew up, almost hit the ceiling, and came right back down. When it hit the table, he slammed his hand down at the same moment. We all jumped out of our skins, and then he said, "You people need to do this *now* and stop wasting my time!" We were all shocked and a little rattled. The prospect jumped up from the table and told us, "Get out!" We did.

That incident left a lasting impression on me—a very talented salesman let his frustrations take over and he made a crucial mistake. As a result, he lost the sale.

LIFE LESSON:
No matter how frustrating a situation gets, you simply cannot, under any circumstances, let it get to you.

Welcome Change

By necessity a salesman must wear many hats. When you are in sales you cannot be afraid to reinvent yourself; you have to be a quick-change artist, adapt to your clients' needs, and be attuned to their emotions in order to make the sale. As a matter of fact, this holds true in business as a whole: you must make changes often and adapt to the times. It is human nature to cling to the known and shy away from the unknown, but in order to grow and expand, the services and products must change to match the shifting times. It can be scary—but more often than not, change will be for the better and will allow you to expand your horizons and grow your business.

Change is all in your mind. Many people tend to think that change creates extra work, when in fact this is not normally true. Of course it takes a bit of time on your part to adapt, but that does not mean that the process as a whole will be more work. Once you are accustomed to it, it will become like second nature. "Short-term pain for long-term gain" is the saying that fits. Change comes more easily when you don't resist it. Change is inevitable and resisting it will not stop change from happening. Once you have adapted to the changes, you will often look back and appreciate the new processes, products, or services. You will be better able to recognize and appreciate the benefits once you've become accustomed to them. Salespeople can very often become entrenched in their ways and be resistant to change, but if you can be an agent of "what's next," your flexibility will allow you greater financial success.

One of the best books about adapting to change is *Who Moved My Cheese?* by Spencer Johnson. It will be a quick read and you will see yourself in one, if not all, of the characters. This book is highly recommended by many successful business people, and I also find it extremely useful.

LIFE LESSON:
Change is inevitable.
If you fight it, you will be left behind, lose money, and be out of the loop.

Get Inspired

Getting a periodic dose of inspiration can be essential to your sales career. Throughout our careers, we can easily become lazy or burned-out, take a few shortcuts, or find ourselves in a slump. It creeps up on us slowly, and though we find ourselves denying that it is happening, we are very clearly not at the top of our game. We typically will try to find a way to justify it by saying that sales are down because of the economy, inflation, weather, holidays, you name it—more likely than not it has been used as an excuse.

Whether or not these are legitimate reasons isn't as important as the fact that you are not bringing in revenue. You have to get over it and get out of the blame game so you can make money. The best way to do that is to *start talking differently* about the circumstances. People often create a wide variety of circumstances just so they don't have to go to work. We recruit what we think are self-motivated, top-quality players who want to make a difference in their lives and the lives of their clients. Unfortunately, some will create issues or circumstances that prevent them from starting off on the right foot, let alone succeeding in their career as sales professionals. A conversation like that will go something like this:

Prospective Employee: Mr. McIntyre, I have several loose ends to tie up before I can get in for training.

Me: Like what?

Prospective Employee: Well, I have this partner who has been stealing me blind, and I have to get my son enrolled in Duke.

Me: Wait a minute, do you have a trust fund? Or is your wife an heiress? I thought you needed to *make* money.

Prospective Employee: Oh, I do! No, my wife isn't rich, but I do have to go get her from work now, so I will call you when wind things down.

At this point, he's lost the job because his potential employer does not believe in his motivation or ability to do the job.

LIFE LESSON:
If you want the job, make yourself available.
There are one hundred other people out there who will happily take your place.

Inspiration can come from many sources. You may look up to great sports figures such as Michael Jordan or Lance Armstrong, or perhaps by an actor, columnist, or political leader. Ronald Reagan's speeches, integrity, and dedication inspired many people, myself among them. His ability to get things done and his no-nonsense, take-no-prisoners style of leadership was inspirational. When President Reagan was shot, he joked at the hospital prior to going in for surgery, "I hope you are all Republicans." *That* was inspirational. He didn't ponder being a victim; he was a leader and stayed focused on his commitment, not the circumstances that surrounded him. Ronald Reagan's speech at Pointe du Hoc, France, in 1984, marking the fortieth anniversary of D-Day, was particularly inspiring:

We stand on a lonely, windswept point on the northern shore of France. The air is soft, but forty years ago at this moment, the air was dense with smoke and the cries of men, and the air was filled with the crack of rifle fire and the roar of cannon. At dawn, on the morning of the sixth of June, 1944, 225 Rangers jumped off the British landing craft and ran to the bottom of these cliffs. Their mission was one of the most difficult and daring of the invasion, to climb these sheer and desolate cliffs and take out the enemy guns.

The Rangers looked up and saw the enemy soldiers at the edge of the cliffs shooting down at them with machine guns and throwing grenades. And the American Rangers began to climb. They shot rope ladders over the face of these cliffs and began to pull themselves up. When one Ranger fell, another would take his place. When one rope was cut, a Ranger would grab another and begin his climb again. They climbed, shot back, and held their footing. Soon, one by one, the Rangers pulled themselves over the top, and in seizing the firm land at the top of these cliffs, they began to seize back the continent of Europe. Two hundred and twenty-five came here. After two days of fighting, only ninety could still bear arms.

These are the boys of Pointe du Hoc. These are the men who took the cliffs. These are the champions who helped free a continent. These are the heroes who helped end a war.

These words inspire me!

LIFE LESSON:
Great inspiration does not have to
be a life-altering moment. It can come from
anywhere or anything at anytime.

Never Stop Training

If you want to be successful in your business life, you must take responsibility for your own training. Don't expect others to be responsible for making you successful. Some companies actually have a great training or "on-boarding" program, but you should not rely on that to be your only training. Seek out your own training to supplement whatever your company offers. There are many resources for this type of training and it is up to you to find them.

Find the top guns in your area and ask to ride along on a few calls. Many companies already do this as common practice in order to ensure that their new hires start out on the right foot and represent the company in the best possible way. You have more than likely seen this before when sitting down to a meal in a restaurant—first the server introduces him or herself and then introduces the trainee. When you are fortunate enough to do a ride-along, be aware of a few important rules. Listen to your trainer and do *exactly* as they say. Keep the modifications of the program until you have mastered the program. Your trainer has been there and done that, so take advantage of that and learn from their experience.

A few years ago I was responsible for training a new recruit. We were driving to an appointment and I was explaining what was going to happen. I told him that I was happy for him to join in the warm-up's small talk but requested that he remain quiet during my presentation. He responded, "I understand, I won't say anything. Don't worry, I have been doing this for a long time."

During the presentation the client asked a question that I wanted to answer later at a more opportune time. I would use it at the right time to close the sale. The trainee interrupted me, "Michael, I think the question he is asking is a valid concern. He wants to know why—"

I stopped him and said, "David, I understand. As agreed earlier, let's hold all of *your* questions for our ride home." He got the message and remained silent the rest of the presentation.

It's hard when you are a trainee and truly think that you can help close the sale; however, you *must* be quiet and observe. Take notes, write down your questions on technique and product knowledge, but do *not* bring up your questions or concerns in front of the client unless the trainer does. You will have plenty of time to ask questions after the presentation in private with your trainer.

Study your product and know your competition, your presentation, typical objections, and how to overcome each of them. Practice and role-play with your spouse, friends, or coworkers.

If you are not in a directly sales-oriented part of the company such as customer service, or are in a support group for sales, like supplies or shipping, it is crucially important for you to know your products and do your research. You are the support group for sales; you are the person customers will go to with their questions and concerns. As such, you need to know the ins and outs of the products in order to provide knowledgeable answers to their questions or to solve their problems. With information available so easily you need to do a great deal of research on the company, products, and the competition. If you truly want to succeed and move up the in ranks of the company, then do the things others either will not do or just don't want to do in order to stand out in a good way. Go above and beyond.

Regardless of whether you plan on being with the company for a short period of time or how low on the totem pole you feel, if you are ambitious, you will want to make your mark at *every* step in your career path. Making those marks will help you succeed and will show people you encounter throughout your career that you are serious, go above and beyond, and are someone they want on their team. Even if something better comes along, it is important to be professional and give proper notice to your employer. Never blow off a job or be disrespectful; it is important to give your job 100 percent to the very end. Don't burn your bridges, because you never know when you will need to cross them again. You may never come back to that particular company, but you also never know who you will work for later in life or where your contacts from that company will work in the future.

When it comes to basic training, you will find a select few people in your company who are not turkeys but eagles—people who want to differentiate themselves. Seek them out and work with them. The Bible says that iron sharpens iron, so get sharp!

LIFE LESSON:
Understand and accept that you
do not know everything. Recognize what you
do not know, accept that, and find the best
people who you can to learn from.
Accept advice and constructive criticism
and adapt it to work for you.

Resort Training

Most people love to go to a resort. Just the word "resort" has a sound of elegance, success, opulence, rest, and relaxation. So why would we need training for this? You don't—you need to have your training *sessions* there!

Make no mistake, the price tag for good training is high, but the cost of poor or no training is catastrophic! One of the greatest teachers, Zig Ziglar himself, once said that there is a big difference between the *price* of something and the *cost* of something.

Allow me to explain this secret of closing the sale as shared by this master of sales. If you want to buy a bicycle and are looking only for a good price then it's easy—you will purchase the cheapest one on the market that looks like what you want. Inevitably it will break. By the time you have had it repaired and been unable to use it while said repairs were being carried out, the cost of the cheap bike you purchased is greater than the most expensive alternative at the time of purchase.

Training is the same way. If you are in management, this is addressed to you. If you are an independent contractor looking to better yourself in your profession, then this is for you, too. You have to invest in your company and yourself in order to grow and succeed. Companies will often wait to see if you are worth your salt before they invest thousands of training dollars on you. Most sales people who are successful understand this. Like the Bible says in the book of Matthew 7, "Do not throw your pearls before swine."

The training atmosphere is very important; you must have a well-thought-out curriculum, it must be rehearsed, and it must be entertaining as well. There is nothing worse than having someone drone on for hours on end. If you are that person, you've lost your audience within the first two minutes of your presentation, and getting them back will be next to impossible. You are competing for people's attention, and you really have to make your training different from all the other noise in their lives. When it comes to training you have two key components for success:

1. The Surrounding Environment: Have you walked into a Holiday Inn or a Best Western hotel? Most of us have, and some of us have been fortunate enough to have walked into a Four Seasons or a Ritz-Carlton. Notice the different images you have in your mind's eye in regard to each hotel. Well, this effect is heightened when you stay there for a training session. Not all companies have the resources of the Ritz, but you would be surprised to find that an upgrade to a Hilton, Westin, or Hyatt isn't that much more expensive than the Motel Six or the Comfort Inn—and believe me, the *cost* will be much cheaper in the long run!

2. Experiential Training: When you learn how to brush your teeth, tie your shoes, or ride your bike, you have used experiential learning. These are skills we don't forget, even if we don't use them for many years; they become ingrained in us. To get the true bang for your buck, I recommend using experiential learning for at least 75 percent of the overall training. There are several different ways to go about this. A couple of examples to use:

   a. Dyads

      - Have your team break up into pairs and face one another without a table or anything in between them. At first participants will be a bit reluctant, but if you set it up right, it will flow easily. Have one of them start by tapping the other on the leg (you always have one person who is not paying attention). Then assign each person as partner A or partner B. Partner A will go first and will explain to partner B the reason why they should buy a certain car. Tell them that they have five minutes to make their presentation. After this have partner A share their experience. Not all will volunteer but enough will, and you should let two or three explain their experience. Ask partner B to explain what they heard (again, two or three should share and then you should move on). Then tell partner B that it is his turn; however, this time try to convince partner A to move to Detroit.

- The whole point of an exercise like this is to lighten the mood, open all their senses for leaning, and help combat the number one problem in business: a lack of effective communication. You can do countless dyads. One of the most effective is to have loud music playing when a person is trying to sell something.

b. Videotaping or Role-Playing

- Videotaping and role-playing are two more great ways to train. You can have cards prepared for each scenario. Have two volunteers act as customers and one person play the salesman. (This could also be done in a management teaching or HR situation.) Have the scenarios written on three-by-five cards for each participant—they should relate to your product or circumstances. The participants will act the situation out, taking around fifteen minutes for each scenario. Afterward, have Q&A time with the audience about what they did right and what they did wrong. These sessions are great tools for learning.

- Have break-out group exercises in which the groups must come up with a solution to a problem and have the group elect one person to present their solution. Generally, if you have the same problem for each group it is very interesting to see the creativity of the various solutions and the leaders that emerge from the groups.

- Depending on how much time is available during the training (a training of two days and one night is recommended at the minimum, with three days and two nights being preferred for team-building purposes), it is important to have a period during the training—most likely at night—for socializing in order to bring people out of their comfort zones. This can be done with a "stretch." A stretch is a skit that makes the group step out of their comfort zone and get past their inhibitions and everyday activities.

c. Stretches

- A stretch is set up by selecting smaller groups, with usually five to eight people per group. (If you have more than fifty people you might consider breaking into two larger groups before branching off into your smaller sections.) The preparation for this activity is very important: you must have the stretches thought out beforehand. The only rule you will have on this is time—no more than twenty minutes per skit. It usually is a lot of fun and great way to let the attendees be creative and learn. When people enjoy learning, the lessons are retained far longer.

3. Great Resources: Having a keynote or motivational speaker is very important as well. Yes, they can be expensive, but you must invest in your number one resource—your people. Having a quality resource can add an opening tone for the whole training experience. It's a great way to get their hearts and heads open for a truly beneficial learning experience.

Closing with a graduation, award ceremony, or banquet is also nice. It's a time for recognition, laughter, and true bonding. If you do it right you should get compliments like, "This was the best training ever!" Or, "This is a game-changer, not only in my career but for my life!" I am serious about this—it makes a *huge* difference in your bottom line and you also get to make a difference in their lives. Truly a win-win!

Resort training takes planning. It is not difficult to organize if you have hired the right people to do it, nor is it as expensive as you might think. It is not always recommended to hand off this task to the administrative staff. Ideally you can hand off the job to the marketing or event-planning teams, who will work along with your national sales manager. Each detail needs to be planned and choreographed; all eventualities should have solutions formulated and ready to put into action. The room in which each training session is to be held is also extremely important, from the setup of the chairs to the lighting to places where people will eat. If you plan your resort training well, it will be an opportunity for team-building and learning that will profit your bottom line for years to come. You must build value into this type of training as well; resort training should be limited to the people that will be with your company for the long haul. When this is done right you will give your employees a source for a new and inspired attitude and method of working.

If you are fortunate enough to attend such training, my advice to you is to go all out! Be authentic, learn from everyone, and share your experiences. You will find that when you share personal stories—failures, triumphs, and all—it will allow you to find encouragement where you might least expect it. It is the law of giving. It's a cool thing. After all, if you're attending resort training, you're probably in the top 5 percent in your company.

Calculate Risk

Life is a risky business, yet many of us choose not to take any risks. One of my favorite quotes is from Teddy Roosevelt: "Far better it is to dare mighty things, to win glorious triumphs, even though checkered by failure, than to take rank with those poor spirits who neither enjoy much nor suffer much, because they live in the gray twilight that knows neither victory nor defeat."

I would rather take a shot at something incredible than not take the risk and regret it later. Of course, you shouldn't take an uncalculated risk—but ironically, you must be careful even in this regard. If you overanalyze everything, you can get frozen in too many "what-ifs."

As an example, look at the world of academia, where we place a huge emphasis on the importance of grades. As parents, we all want our children to get good grades; however, that should not be our principal goal. Much of the world of academia looks at things with a different perspective than the creative entrepreneur or the risk-taker. Bill Gates never finished college, and many CEOs started out in the lowest rung of the company ladder with a bachelor's degree or less, but they all worked hard and created opportunities for themselves—they took risks.

Jack Welch, former CEO of General Electric, started out as chemical engineer and blew up an entire plastics factory. Michael Eisner, former CEO of Disney, started out as a page at NBC and was eventually hired at ABC—where he took a risk on a young Italian actor and cast him in *Welcome Back, Kotter* in the early '70s. Several years later he cast that actor in a new style of film that no one wanted to make. It was a low-budget movie and he put his reputation on the line at Paramount Pictures, but it turned out to be a huge success. That movie was *Grease,* starring two relatively unknown actors: John Travolta and Olivia Newton-John.

The point is that you cannot be timid; you must put yourself out there. The *only* way you will be highly successful is to take risks, and when you fail (and make no mistake, you will fail sometimes) you must go right back at it again. Whatever you do, don't quit. As President Calvin Coolidge said, "Nothing in this world can take the place of persistence. Talent will not; nothing is more common than unsuccessful people with talent. Genius will not; unrewarded genius is almost a proverb. Educations will not; the world is full of educated derelicts. Persistence and determination alone are omnipotent."

Many people overanalyze the deal. If you start to get into three or more what-if scenarios, you are overanalyzing the situation. To avoid this, anytime you are considering a new career, an idea for a business, an investment, or anything that could be life-changing, get a second or third opinion from people you trust. Let them know up front why you are calling a meeting. Be sure to let them know that you are not looking for an investor. Don't be surprised if they tell you that your baby is ugly ("your baby" being your business idea or new career). Defend it, however, if you truly believe in it. It's much cheaper and less painful if they point out something to you that you totally missed because you caught the fever of your visions of grandeur. On the other hand, you may be spot-on, have a great idea or a huge opportunity, and you simply needed reassurance from those you trust.

Many of us are afraid to share our dreams or ambitions. We do not want to look foolish, and because of that fear, we either don't act or don't ask. It's OK to ask for help; it's OK not to know *everything*. We all have vast amounts of networking that can trigger an idea, or someone can make a phone call to connect you with that supplier you need. More often than not you are just three degrees of separation from help and answers. Frequently all you need is the validation that will give you the confidence you seek so that you feel you can take that risk.

Deal with the Ups and Downs . . .

A perfect world doesn't exist. We all know this, but we have all had days when life seemed incredibly easy. You get to your appointment five minutes ahead of schedule, the directions are easy to follow, and the people are expecting you. They are tidily presented and ready to welcome you—they are truly *interested* in what you're coming to sell them. You make your presentation, they love it, they buy your product, and you leave that perfect prospect (now your new client) feeling on top of the world. You realize you have time on your hands, so you head down to the local satellite office (a.k.a the nearest Denny's restaurant) and order a pot of coffee while you clean up your paperwork and savor your latest victory.

This is all wonderful, but just yesterday you had two no-shows and a "broke" (a customer with no money); you were almost ready to quit. So you thank the sales gods for their generosity, finish your paperwork, and get ready for your next appointment. This is the tipping point! Once you get the spark, you can easily catch fire. The world seems a little bit brighter, your problems don't seem so insurmountable, and you have a little pep in your step. You get to your next appointment and though they are home, they are not quite as receptive as your last appointment. However, you have garnered more confidence from your earlier sale, so you close this one as well. It was a great presentation with a good, solid close. You used the Five-Point Close and it worked perfectly. Now you're back; you're on a roll. For the next few weeks you continue to do really well, even breaking all your personal records.

This happens all the time—the trick is to hang in there when things aren't going your way. Have confidence and belief in your abilities. If you have the talent, the work ethic, the knowledge, and the burning desire to make a difference, the good times can and will come around. The spark will come and the fire will catch. Know it and enjoy it. You deserve it.

. . . And the Not-So-Perfect

At some point in your career you're going to get discouraged or have a truly tough day. People deal with "bad days" differently. Below are a few techniques that have been effective with helping me get through the bad times.

First I have to vent. My wife has listened to me do so too many times to count. As I unleash these pent-up frustrations, I get on a roll and start bringing up issues from previous deals as well. When I'm venting, my wife looks at me and says "OK, Michael, you can run this for another ten minutes and you get to be angry for the next hour, then get over it and move on." This is exactly what I try to do.

Sales—especially straight commission sales—can sometimes get very dicey. I believe you really need a good outlet; sharing your frustrations, your fears, and your concerns with someone you trust is so important. My faith plays a huge role in my life, not only as an anchor to hold on to in the storms that come, but also in the good times for gratitude and praise when the sky is blue and the wind is at my back. Delving into scripture often helps me reaffirm my faith and find solutions to the problems that I might be facing.

The second thing that helps me is going to the movies. Movies, especially in the middle of a really bad day, help me gain perspective. I find that it can be very therapeutic just to forget about my problems or frustrations for a couple of hours. Moreover, not only are movies a great two-hour escape, they often can be quite inspirational.

Not too long ago I was having a challenging day, so I went to the movies. Later that evening, my family and I were discussing the events of our days. I said, "Well, Daddy's day had a lot of frustrating moments, so I decided to go to the movies." My youngest daughter asked me how I did that. She wanted to know why I didn't have to ask someone for permission. I explained that I owned the company and therefore have a lot of responsibilities that sometimes get very frustrating and stressful, so I need an escape to figure out how to fix some problems. Her response was, "Wow! You have a great life. I wish I could just go to the movies whenever I wanted to."

She was spot-on! I *do* have a great life—even if sometimes I'm staring at the ceiling at two in the morning, wondering if a new deal will work. Sometimes you just need a little perspective to set your head straight again.

Learn from Your Mistakes

Here is a short list of the some of the mistakes I have made so far. Of course, I will continue to make mistakes, because I will continue to take risks and I will always strive to move forward. If you are just getting into a new career, whatever it may be, take note. Here are a few missteps I wish I had been warned about early on, as well as a bit of general advice that I wish someone had given to me.

Don't Get a Big Head

One of the biggest mistakes that any salesperson can make is becoming overconfident. When I first started I was very enthusiastic and focused. I had one mission—make the sale and make another sale. A manager told me early on that I am only as good as my *next* sale, and that stuck with me. For the first six months in my sales career I set records and won a gold watch, a new car, and a trip. I was on *fire!* I had no idea how well I was doing until my first sales convention.

I went to the awards banquet and won a lot of prizes; in fact, I tied with the top producers in the company. So of course, I caught the "Big Head Disease" over the next few weeks and started believing everything everyone was telling me. I wanted to be the *best* so I started to study the product in detail and gained a vast amount of knowledge, which was good. However, what was not so great was my attempt to pass *all* that knowledge on to my prospects, overwhelming them and often losing the sale.

Before I knew that I was "good" at sales, I gave *everyone* my very best presentation. After I knew I was a "super salesman," I figured I could coast a little—*big mistake!* My sales plummeted. I didn't manage to pull out of that downward spiral until I discovered the Five-Point Close.

You *do* need confidence in your presentation, your product, and yourself. What you *don't* need is to be *over-*confident and try to take shortcuts—the only shortcut you will find is the one to the poor house.

Stay on the Top of Your Game

Check yourself often and remember that you can *always* learn. Ride along with a respected sales colleague and have them listen to your presentation. Record your presentation (a painful but effective process). Go to sales seminars, read books, study your profession. Always improve yourself; *never stop learning.* This will keep you both grounded and growing.

Don't Spend All Your Money

When I first started in sales, I saved some of my commissions for a while, but then I started to spend them. I loaned money that normally wasn't paid back. I got a taste for the good life and went a little overboard.

In straight commission sales (where I believe the most success can be found), if you are not making a presentation, you are unemployed. Reward yourself, but also be conservative and save for the rainy days. They will come, trust me.

Don't Count Your Chickens Before They Are Hatched

A client can cancel a contract, and if you have already spent the commissions and bragged to colleagues, you'll not only look like a fool, you'll likely have some financial issues to deal with as well. Then one of two things usually happens: the sales rep either leaves or takes the blow, chalks it up to experience, climbs back on the horse, and starts again. Most leave.

I've counted my chickens on more than one occasion, and I've learned that the sale is not done until the client says it's done. For this reason, you have to maintain your focus and persevere. Many new salespeople, myself included, think that once you get the check or the order, it's over. In reality, this is when the real work begins—big commissions are great, but big refunds or charge-backs are embarrassing and can wreak havoc on your checking account. So you need to keep on selling. As a matter of fact, you shouldn't count a transaction as complete until the client is satisfied and the commissions are in the bank. Keep selling. Five clients worth $10,000 are better for your bottom line than one client worth the same amount of money.

Make sure your eyes are wide-open. When you start tasting success in sales, don't relax—keep working. Look at all possible eventualities, including the worst-case scenarios, and make your decisions carefully. Hope for the best but plan for the unexpected. Always keep a reserve on hand just in case.

Learn from Your Successes

If we can admit our mistakes, own them, and learn from them, we can savor our successes even more. It does not matter whether we earn our success after walking through the fire of our mistakes or if our success comes naturally—as long as those things that we do right are things that help us propel our career forward. Remember that what we think is right for us isn't always right for everyone.

We've looked at some of my mistakes above; now let's examine a few of my successes.

Be Observant and Decisive

I knew from an early age what I did *not* want to do or become. I knew I didn't want to wring my hands over bills, trying to make ends meet. I knew I didn't want to go through a painful divorce.

I also knew what I *did* want. At a very young age, I knew that I liked steak, nice clothes, and the respect certain people were given when they went into a nice restaurant. I was about nine years old when I knew I loved the thrill of almost winning it all in a bingo tournament. In short, I knew that I wanted to be successful, respected, and never have to want for anything.

Around age eight, I remember making a clear, conscious commitment to enjoy the finer things life had to offer. In that regard, one of the first things I did right was to *observe*—to pay attention to my surroundings and take mental notes of outcomes of various situations.

Be Awake to Take Advantage of All Opportunities

It was 1978 when I went into the air force. Back then, as long as you could turn your head and cough, you were in. I signed up for college as soon as I could, which was one of the best things I did in the military. The military encouraged us to go to school and would even give students time off from duty to study. If I hadn't gone into the military, I would not have gotten a higher education. It was a great opportunity and the smart recruits seized it.

That said, it wasn't an easy road by any means. It required a great deal of sacrifice and discipline. Many times my fellow airmen were bowling, going to ball games, or golfing, while I was spending my time off stuck in the classroom or studying. You see, we had full-time jobs in the air force, so there was no slacking.

Take advantage of all opportunities that come your way, even if you are unsure of the benefit—you never know what good they might do for you further down the road.

Spend Time with Your Family

Everyone knows the validity of the saying "quality over quantity," but I believe that there is one very important exception—your family. How can you determine what qualifies as "quality time" with one's family? Instead, you must focus on quantity—huge amounts of it. Sometimes your time with your family will be spent doing special things; often it will be more routine. It's simply the act of spending time *together* that matters.

One night we were at dinner with all three of our daughters, discussing the usual highs and lows of our days.

One of our older girls had opened a bank account, and we asked how much she had saved. The youngest, who was about ten at the time, was very aware of how much money she had and was very competitive about saving more than her sisters. She began to ask her sisters about their stashes, and it wasn't long before it occurred to her to ask how much Stacye and I had saved. My point is that an ordinary family dinner turned into a humorous family memory—one we were able to make simply because we were spending time together.

Have a Good Work Ethic

I learned from my parents, who both have strong work ethics that drive them to get up and get going. Start early and work late. They also taught me to work smarter not harder, though hard work will always be an important part of the equation.

Delegation is a key component of "working right." You must know what you are good at and find others to do the things that you don't do well; this enables you to focus on your strengths. For example, I am good at making the sales, but I'm not particularly adept at administration, so I hired the best administrative person I could find. This is where a lot of *good* salespeople could become *great*—if they would part with a dollar and hire someone to perform the tasks they are not good at doing. You will be amazed at your return on investment. Don't be penny-wise and dollar-foolish.

Follow-up is another characteristic that is vital to your continued success. If you say you're going to do something, do it. Keep a note pad or a small tape recorder with you and make a to-do list. Each day, scratch off the things you've accomplished and add the new "to-dos." This will keep you on point for follow-through. How often do we tell someone, "I will send you that book," but get distracted and forget do so? Then the next time we see that person, we snap our fingers, and say "Joe, I'm sorry, I intended to get that for you—I forgot." This makes you seem unprofessional and disorganized. Write it down and follow-through. Learn this mantra: "If it isn't written down, it does not exist."

When you call on a prospect or a client and you have followed through on your promise, your credibility goes straight up. You will make more sales and get more referrals than ever. It takes work and commitment—that big *C* word—but it's most definitely worth it.

Part 3
Homework

Telling a story is a great way to help your prospect visualize themselves with your product or service. If you don't have any stories of your own yet, it's OK to borrow someone else's—just be sure to cite the source.

Think of a story related to your profession or your product. Like all parts of your presentation, your story must be well-rehearsed and well-researched. Do *not* wing it.

_____

_____

_____

_____

_____

_____

You'll want to create some of your own narratives. You never know when a well-timed story can make all the difference and seal the deal.

_____

_____

_____

_____

_____

_____

_____

_____

_____

_____

_____

_____

_____

Part 4

The Presentation

seven

Preparing for the Presentation

The Drift

"The Drift" is a state of consciousness or unconsciousness; it's a way of thinking that we were born into; it's what we think as we walk around each day. We were born into this way of operating and taught this from a young age. Metaphorically, it's the water in which we swim; it's the way we see things. Those aware of the Drift do not settle for the status quo or for being good enough—you always try to better yourself. You are aware of the Drift and are rarely pulled into it; when you are, you are able recognize it and dislodge yourself from it.

The Drift basically has three parts that one must recognize in order to understand it and sell into it. Those three characteristics are:

1. Being right

2. Being in control

3. Looking good

As a note, when I say "looking good," I do not mean your physical appearance, though that does play a part as well. I mean looking like you are in control even when you aren't. It's about the appearance of things.

Those who can successfully navigate the Drift can readily recognize it, know that it is present, and deal with it. Look at the movie *The Matrix*; coming out of the Drift is similar to when Keanu Reeves sees the world as it really is. It turns out that we make up interpretations of what we see, do, and experience. We think that this is because of another person or circumstance rather than our lifetime of conditioning. In our interactions with others, we have buttons that we allow other people to push, which then provoke a strong reaction in or from us. Knowing how and why—that is, becoming aware of ourselves—is the first step to navigating and recognizing the Drift. At that "ah-ha" point you will be *much* more able to successfully handle life's variety of situations.

Being Right

We will do almost anything to be right. We will lose lifelong relationships, we will get divorced, and we will go to war. We will protest, condemn, lose our health, and of course, we will judge. Why is it so important to us to be right? Many psychologists say that if we are right about something, we can then deny reality and therefore deny the ultimate finish—death. I know this is very heavy, so let's lighten it up a little.

When you are in a romantic relationship, especially during the courting stage, the drive to be right goes out the window, particularly if it could be a serious relationship. Why is that? Well, we are focused on our main goal, which is them falling for us the same way we are falling for them.

Trivial things like them chewing with their mouth open, cracking their knuckles, or even smoking cigarettes don't matter at the time. We simply let those things be, ignoring the habits which most annoy us.

After we have reached the goal, things start to change; we get pickier and more agitated about those things because we are not focused on the prize any longer. Instead, we are focused on our need to be right—even about how the other person should behave. Then one day, after ten years of marriage, you wake up and say, "I have had it with you! I'm mad as hell, and I am not going to take this anymore!"

Statistically, more than 50 percent of marriages end in divorce. This is usually because one or both parties in the relationship are insisting on being right. Please don't misunderstand this: if someone is in an abusive relationship of any sort, it's not about being right, it's about being safe and getting help immediately.

We can take this knowledge and apply it to our relationships with our children, coworkers, patients, clients, and prospects. Think about it: You are frightened about a presentation or you are challenged about your product. Even worse, you're challenged about your integrity or profession. Most of us have an innate tendency to defend ourselves. We want to be right; we need to convince our prospect, client, child, or spouse that we are right. We may win the argument but ultimately, we lose a little something of ourselves and a great deal in our client or prospect's eyes—or worst of all, in our personal relationships.

Step back for a minute and take a 180-degree look through the other person's eyes, even if the facts are on your side. You will gain a 360-degree perspective and understand where you need to come from to serve both yourself and the other person. A conversation involving this technique may go something like this:

> **Customer:** I don't think this will help us at all. These widgets are overpriced and take twice as long to implement.

> **Salesman:** I totally understand your concern and you are right—it is expensive.

Now what do you think the prospect is thinking? Something along the lines of, "Wow! This guy is on my side!" The customer feels heard and understood. From there you can bring some new ideas into the conversation and presentation.

In personal relationships, there is much more emotional attachment involved. We have years of buttons that have been pushed, manipulated, and twisted. In these types of situations, we tend to be much more invested in being right. However, if you understand that your wife, husband, and child want to be right and in control as well, you can then deal with the situation in a more loving and caring way, often avoiding hurtful arguments.

What there is to learn from this characteristic of the Drift is that we *all* want to be right. If the other person is right then they get to feel in control. If you can let this happen, you may find that you can *both* be right!

Being in Control

The second characteristic—being in control—refers to fear. Most of us experience fear when we lose control of a situation. How do you feel flying in an airplane at thirty-five thousand feet in a thunderstorm at night? Many of us are acutely aware of how little control we have over the situation and we feel afraid. We may get nervous and anxious, or get a bad case of dry mouth or sweaty palms. We may envision newspaper headlines such as PLANE LOSES CONTROL, CRASHES, KILLING ALL ABOARD. This is where we may get mad at those around us, blaming them; in truth, they are no more in control than we are at that particular moment—it's not the crew's fault. The weather is not within their control. Are you able to control yourself and your emotions and work your way to the other side? If not, you will need to find a way to do so if you have any intention of being successful in life. Fight or flight—which one are you going to do? You may not be in control of the situation, but you can be in control of yourself.

This happens on the ground as well: we get called in to see the boss, receive mail from the IRS, or are served a lawsuit. In a sales career, it is even more important to understand the Drift and be able to navigate your way through it. Let's say, for example, that you are in a slump or are having a bad week in sales, not quite performing the way you normally would. When challenged about this for whatever reason (justified or not), we usually start the "blame game." It goes something like this:

Manager: Jeff, I really think your performance the past month has been subpar. I am concerned and do not want you to leave the company. What do we need to do to get you back on track?

Jeff: Well, it's not any single problem. You see, my leads have not been any good. None of these leads

In this scenario, Jeff blamed the leads, implying that his poor performance was not his fault. He was not in control of this reprimand but tried desperately to gain control of the situation by diverting the attention away from himself and blaming his circumstances rather than his own ineptness or inability.

We tend to have a strong need to be in control—in command of our money, our relationships, our careers, and, well, everything, right? Raising three daughters taught me that I truly am not in control of very much. I can stack the odds in my favor most of the time, but even then Murphy's Law will kick in and *WAM!* I lose the control.

Being in control is the cornerstone of the Drift because once you learn that none of us are really in control of anything, the other components of the Drift make complete sense. If after your next presentation, review, or meeting, you leave your audience feeling that they are not in total control of the process you are presenting, your message is less likely to have the intended result.

I have seen very talented presenters and salespeople walk into a situation and find themselves intimidated for some unexpected reason. They may see a person they find very attractive; maybe the surroundings are very posh and sophisticated; or on the other hand, perhaps the surroundings are a bit sketchy and that causes some fear, issues, or memories from the past to surface. Many things may trigger the "out of control" feeling.

When cruising at thirty-five thousand feet in a thunderstorm, people often go on the offensive and verbally attack each other for no apparent reason. In reality, it is because they feel that they are not in control. In addition, some of us have learned that if we are rude and aloof we can regain control of the situation. As a result, others feel diminished—which they don't like at all. They then shut down faster than Three Mile Island in an accident.

You are probably wondering how to identify when you're in the Drift and how can you get out of it. The answer is this: be aware that you are upset, then be authentic and honest with yourself. This is very important. You can go out there and fool them some of the time but not all of the time. The real value is in no longer fooling yourself—or at any rate, doing so as little as possible.

Remember that God loves you no matter what. You have individual characteristics that make you unique, and that is something to celebrate. Lying to yourself will not serve you or those around you well at all. Learning to control yourself will help you release any insecurity and allow you to make the most of what life brings your way. You can then deal with any problem. Pray on it, talk to a trusted advisor, do whatever you need to do. Deal with it in your own way, then own it and let it go. That way, the next time you face an intimidating situation you will be able to recognize it and handle it. You may still have some of those feelings pop up, but you will be able to operate differently.

I therefore recommend that you become aware of this main aspect of the Drift and its hold on you. The recognition of this fact is essential to your success and your ability to help your clients achieve their goals.

Looking Good

The Drift has a very strong current. Most likely you woke up this morning, brushed your teeth, and washed and styled your hair. You then looked in your closet and decided what to wear. Ninety-five percent of us want to "look good" in whatever way we define that. The Drift tells us that we must have certain shoes, purses, belts, and so on. We must weigh a certain amount, drive a certain car, and live in a certain neighborhood. All of this is the superficial side of looking good. An overwhelming sense of fashion is not imperative, but you need to understand that that you both feel better and look better to prospects if you are well groomed, your clothes fit, and your teeth are clean.

The problem comes when physical appearance is *all* we care about. This characteristic is an integral part of the other two aspects of the Drift, especially the need to be in control. Have you ever showed up at a function underdressed or overdressed? You feel a little self-conscious, and perhaps your insecurities kick in. Or you think you look good until a Brad Pitt look-alike shows up and you start to play the comparison game—you will lose, so don't play. Remember that you are the way you are for a reason; God made you special. If in fact you feel that you could use some fashion coaching, then get it, but be careful not to become obsessed with physical appearance.

Let's move on to looking good in our work life. What happens here is that many of us get nervous when someone says "action," and we sometimes trip or stumble. We then feel as though we look foolish or like we don't know what the heck we are doing—frankly, we feel like idiots.

The fastest way to diffuse these situations is to be vulnerable and retain your integrity. If someone asks you a question to which you don't know the answer, don't fake it. You may want to respond in this way: "I want to apologize. I thought I knew all of the options today that were of interest to you. However, I find myself unprepared to answer that question. It's a great question and I will get the answer for you shortly; I just don't have it now. The last thing I want to do is give you bad information. Please forgive my ignorance."

This is a *much* better response than trying to dance your way around admitting that you don't have the information. Even though you should have known the answer, owning up to your shortcomings will diffuse the situation and your credibility will go up in the client's eyes. The biggest irony about looking good is the fact that most people don't care about what you look like, even though they care a great deal about how they look. It turns out that the main thing that makes you attractive and appealing is your willingness to be vulnerable and authentic. The best speeches at conferences or seminars begin with the keynote speaker saying, "Boy, these lights are really bright. It's a good thing because then I can't see your faces—I am really nervous." We feel immediately connected to that individual because we can totally relate.

USA Today had a poll in which they asked people to name their number one fear. Public speaking ranked first. In second place was death—meaning most of us would *literally* rather die than give a speech in public. Yet when that speaker is scared *and* genuine, we can listen, feel connected to them, and even like them. When you are in business and making a presentation, I urge you to be authentic with your colleague or prospect. *Never* fake it.

There will of course be times in your career when you will have had a difficult day, but it is important to remember that every prospect deserves your very best presentation. You may have to spend some time in short meditation, go to a movie, read scripture, or call your spouse. This will help ground you for your meeting or presentation. It's OK to have a bad day, but do not try to win an Oscar while covering it up; it will make you look bad. Be real and you will ultimately look good without even trying.

Prepare for Your Appointment

If you are in outside sales, it is extremely important to prepare for your appointments, and that involves everything from your tools to your hair. The following are things that we take for granted or overlook as we become comfortable and complacent in our lives and careers.

Appearance

No matter what you look like—short, tall, average, thin, overweight, balding, or with lots of hair—you must look your best. You don't have to be the most beautiful or handsome person in the world to be successful, but you must take care with your appearance. By taking the time to look the best you can, you show your potential clients that you respect them and their time, and you appreciate that they are meeting with you. Your clothes should be ironed and starched; after all, a long day can lead to many wrinkles. You should look as fresh at your last appointment as you did for your first. Your hair should be groomed and your hands and nails clean and manicured. When making presentations it is most professional to do so in a suit and tie. This shows respect for your profession as well as for your audience. Shoes need to be clean and polished. Pay attention to your scent as well as your appearance. Avoid wearing too much perfume or cologne; a little goes a long way, and you do not want to draw attention away from your presentation because your scent is too strong or overwhelming. It is equally important not to smoke. As a smoker you will not notice the overwhelming smell that smoking leaves behind, but the smell lingers and can be offensive to nonsmokers. It leaves a bad impression—and that's something you never want to do.

Appearances don't stop or start with the physical; they extend to your automobile as well. Your car should be clean inside and out. Many times, your automobile will set the stage for your prospect's first impression, and you want to make sure that your first impression is a positive one. While it may sound trivial, avoid eating in your car. Eating while driving makes it much easier to spill something on your clothes, and food can leave an unpleasant odor in your car, which does not leave a good impression if you need to take your client somewhere.

Courtesy

When you drive up to your prospect's house, do *not* park in their driveway unless you are absolutely prohibited from parking anywhere else. You should park at the curb or in a parking lot close to the prospect's home or business. You may have a car that leaks, and you don't want to leave oil or antifreeze on your prospect's driveway as your last impression; you will irritate the client. Don't walk on their grass; use the sidewalk. If you can see the prospect's house when you get out of the car, wave in the direction of the house, even if you cannot see any people. This lets your prospect know that you see them (even though you probably can't) and it sends a friendly message so that your prospect will be more inclined to come to the door. More often than not, if you have a scheduled appointment, you will be expected and they will be waiting for you to arrive.

eight

During the Presentation

Those in outside sales in particular must have a good warm-up session, which helps you prepare for your meeting. Even if you are working in a computer or electronics center, you need to have exceptional people skills. This is something that can be learned; however, a pleasing personality and sense of humor are a good start. What happens if you don't have a great personality? Rent one! Seriously, you can develop your personality and people skills through terrific courses such as Toastmasters, Dale Carnegie, and others. In sales, it's all about communication, which requires listening and verbalizing with excellence, as well as reading between the lines.

A good salesperson knows that no two prospects are the same and that they are influenced by everything from weather to their gender. For example, if you are male and you have an appointment with a husband and wife, after knocking on the door, wait patiently until your prospect answers. Don't have your hands in your pockets and don't fidget. Look at the door and get your head in the game. When the door opens and you see that it's the wife, take one step back and slightly nod your head. Introduce yourself at this time. "Good afternoon, Mrs. Prospect. My name is Michael McIntyre and we have an appointment." Have your picture ID readily available in case she asks for it. This puts your female prospect at ease and shows that you are a gentleman. When she opens the door, wipe your feet on the doormat; if one is not there, go through the motions anyway. This shows respect for her house, which further demonstrates respect for her. Only shake her hand if she offers it to you first. If the husband answers the door, do everything the same way, except you do not need to take a step back and you *do* need to offer to shake his hand.

Once you are in the house it is important to identify with something quite quickly. It could be photographs, military paraphernalia, or evidence of hobbies. Once again, you need to be genuine and be sure not to fake it or your prospects will pick up on your insincerity. Listen to your prospects. More than likely you are not the first salesperson that they have encountered. Ask questions about them: where are they from, how did they meet, how long have they been married, how many children and grandchildren do they have? During this time you need to interject things about yourself as well; this is prime time to establish congeniality and trustworthiness, and that can only be done once the prospect knows something about you. At this time they are getting to know you, too. They want to know about your professional background and sometimes they will even ask about your education and your family.

Be observant without being nosy. Look at your surroundings. Is the TV on? The program they are watching will tell you a lot about your client. Look at the house, the furniture, and their clothing. Are they neat or messy? These are all interesting and relevant facts about your client. You simply must be able to read people as well as read between the lines and make a quick assessment based upon your observations.

Years ago, when I had only been in sales for about four months, I was working for an agency that required its employees to travel frequently. I was assigned to northern Michigan and had an appointment at a country farmhouse. A gentleman of about seventy answered and invited me in. I found myself in a labyrinth of old newspapers stacked to the ceiling; there was just enough space to walk through the rooms. I followed the gentleman through about five turns until it opened up to a small space, just large enough to fit a four-top kitchen table. Seated at the table were his wife and his son. This instantly told me a lot about them: they were very reclusive and private people, and their son was very much a part of their affairs. I introduced myself and the son gave me a firm handshake. The wife had her back to me so I could not yet see her face. When I came around to sit in front of her I saw that she had a huge growth on the side of her face, which I found very disturbing. I felt immediate sympathy for her and then I felt myself becoming nauseous. I did my best not to look shocked and asked if I might use their facilities. The husband was very nice and walked me through the maze to the restroom.

I shut the door and got control of myself. When I felt better I resolved to block it out of my mind and make the best of the situation. I returned to the table and did not look at her during the rest of my presentation. I directed the presentation toward the son because he had a lot of questions. It was a life insurance policy, and he wanted to make sure he would be taken care of when he inherited the farm. As a result of reading my prospects, I made the sale and a very large commission as well. I think I was probably the first salesperson to give them a presentation in a long time and perhaps the only one who had been granted entrance to their home.

The warm-up centers on the small chitchat that you need to make to establish a connection with your prospect. When is the warm-up over? When your prospect says it is over. I assure you they will look at you at some point in the conversation and say, "Michael, let's get to it. I don't have all day to chat. What is this all about anyway?" Every now and then you may get a chatty one, so after about twenty minutes—never more than forty-five minutes—you need to transition into the sales presentation.

Logistics

Logistics are very important as well. I prefer to warm up in the living room or den and move into the kitchen when it's time for business. Making the transition is as simple as standing up and saying to your prospect, "OK, let's move to the kitchen table so I can share these ideas with you." While you say this, begin walking toward the kitchen. Unless you are in a mansion, you should be able to find it fairly easily. In this way you will make a physical transition from the "getting to know you" phase to the "let's get down to business" phase. This might not always happen. Sometimes you will be brought directly to the kitchen table. Don't let it get the best of you; adapt and go with the flow.

If you have to do your warm-up at the kitchen table, that's fine. At the transition point, if they haven't already asked you if you would like something to drink, you might ask them for a glass of water. More than likely they will have already offered you a beverage and perhaps even a cookie or some other snack. You should always take it and at least drink or nibble on the offering. If you are given a choice, it is appropriate to take your cue from your prospect—don't take a bigger helping of food than they do. If you don't like what they have to offer, you can ask for something else, but don't put them out. You can stomach a sip or two of whatever; it won't kill you. However, *never* drink alcohol or smoke with a prospect. It doesn't matter if you just made a gazillion dollars and they want to celebrate. Make a toast but don't drink. Appearances are important, and it is vital to appear responsible.

Positioning

Positioning can be key to making the sale. If you are presenting to a husband and wife in their home, ask if you can all sit at the kitchen table or, failing that, the dining-room table. A table is very important because it will not only act as a makeshift desk, it is also frequently the place the family pays their bills or handles their business. Once you arrive at the table you must take control. Ask the wife to sit at your immediate right (if you are right-handed) and ask her husband sit to *her* immediate right. Do *not* have them sit across from each other if you can avoid it; you want to establish the line of sight to your advantage, not theirs. The seat to your immediate right is the "power" seat; if the wife is next to you, she automatically feels more important in the decision-making process. This also allows you to be more personable with her. Simple gestures and eye contact can go a long way when it comes to gaining someone's trust.

If you are selling to a parent and child, you need to make a judgment call as to who will sit in the "power" seat. Generally, it will be the person you feel will have the biggest influence on the final decision in regard to purchases.

If you're in retail, real estate, car sales, or any type of sales where you are standing and talking to your prospect, you generally need to position yourself at the eleven o'clock– or one o'clock–position in front of the prospect. Slightly off center to the right or left, depending on who you think is in the "power position," is the best setup for you. This will serve the same purpose as the table that we previously discussed. It keeps both of your prospects within your line of sight without offending them by being directly in their path. This positioning allows you to pivot and change direction or stay the course as needed. If you find yourself in an awkward position, don't worry, just deal with it the best you can. Use your tools to extricate yourself.

Do *not* try to force your prospect. Make the seating suggestion once, never more. You may say, "Mr. and Mrs. Prospect, if you don't mind, may I please seat Mrs. Prospect here? Mr. Prospect, you can sit just to the right of your wife. I would really appreciate it. You see, I'm right-handed and it will be easier for you to see what I'm presenting this way." Ninety-nine times out of one hundred they will agree, but if they ignore you or are defiant, you need to concede and find a work-around. Let them feel like they are in the driver's seat, even though you are. If this happens, you will probably need to warm up a little more to gain their trust.

Vocal Inflections

One of the greatest sales books ever written emphasizes the importance of watching your vocal inflections. *Secrets of Closing the Sale*, written by Zig Ziglar, can teach you many things that would otherwise take you many lost sales to learn. Vocal inflections are a part of our everyday life and are something that we do unconsciously.

For instance, take the sentence, "*I* didn't say she stole the money." This one sentence can have seven different meanings by emphasizing each of the separate words: "I *didn't* say she stole the money," indicates that someone else could have said it. "I didn't *say* she stole the money," suggests that maybe I actually did say it. "I didn't say *she* stole the money," means that perhaps I implied that she did rather than said it outright. "I didn't say she *stole* the money," means that it was someone else besides her who stole the money. "I didn't say she stole *the* money," indicates she could have lost it. "I didn't say she stole the money," implies she could have stolen some other money besides that which we are discussing. Finally, "I didn't say she stole the *money*," indicates that she didn't steal the money, but she may have stolen something else.

The way that you stress different words within a sentence can change the meaning entirely and therefore can alter the direction of the conversation. Using different stressors and inflections during a conversation can help you lead the conversation in the direction that you wish it to go and will be of great help to you when using the Five-Point Close techniques.

Setting the Stage

Getting everything straight in your mind is essential to a great warm-up, presentation, and close. When I was in the field doing outside sales, it was not unusual to see salespeople go into a prospect's house either looking as if they were desperate for the sale or acting as if the prospect were doing them a favor. This is not the way to approach a sale. If you believe in your product/service and you have confidence in your abilities, you and your prospect will be better served if you go into the prospect's home with a professional attitude. Your product is great, you are helping them, and you know it; in other words, approach the prospect with a strictly positive attitude.

Think about when you go to see your doctor, attorney, or accountant. It rarely goes like this: "Hi, Michael, thanks for coming in for your checkup. We are very excited to have you as a patient today! In fact, we have some terrific new drugs we really think you are going to enjoy. Now, can we please have you come back again next month and every month for the next year? As a matter of fact, I will call you again on Thursday to see if you want another prescription, or even better, maybe a new X-ray and a CT scan would be good, too! It's awesome and even though it's $2,500, it's great. Do you know anyone else who could benefit from it?" That might be an overexaggeration, but you get the point.

Greet your prospect with integrity and enthusiasm, but know that you are there to *help* them. You have the solution to their problem; you will be the answer to their need. Don't be patronizing or overzealous, be professional. Yes, it is OK to have fun and laugh with your client, but don't force it. Be yourself, knowing you're going to provide a much-needed professional product or service.

Lifelines

Lifelines connect you to people who know the product you're selling. They understand what happens when you are with a prospect and need to know something about your company, your product, your service, or just need some advice when you are "stuck." The ego, however, often stands in the way of asking for help. You must remember that lifelines can help you close the sale, and that is the name of the game, regardless of your ego. It is important to recognize the use and significance of lifelines. I have trained thousands of salespeople on the use of lifelines and after having had them come back to say that lifelines had saved them sale after sale, it's no wonder that they are a highly valued tool for savvy salespeople.

If you are in a sales position where you have outside support of some kind besides your sales manager, you already have built-in lifelines. If you are completely independent, you need to find a lifeline somewhere. You may be able to find a colleague who is in the same sales field with whom you can reciprocate when needed. Whatever your situation, lifelines can help you make sales—and money.

Once you have established your lifelines, you need to know how to use them. If you are in the middle of a presentation and the prospect asks a question that you can't answer, shelve that question until you finish your presentation. Simply say, "Mr. Prospect, that's a great question. I will get to that issue in just a moment." Make a note right then so you won't forget it. Then finish your presentation, and if the prospect isn't already at the point of buying, use a tactic such as this: As you start to broach the subject, be calling your lifeline. At the same time, say, "Mr. Prospect, you asked a question earlier and I want to make sure that I give you accurate information."

The point here is two-fold. First, you are demonstrating that you are a thorough worker. Second, you are showing your prospect that have a support team to assist you—it's not just you, your laptop, and your wife working out of your car. Call your manager, your home office, the manufacturer, or your support team—whoever it is, if they are worth their salt they will have already had extensive training in the support role and will be able to assist you immediately. If not, you have bigger problems (you need to find a new deal).

Once you have your lifeline on the phone, outline the situation briefly. (You *must* be honest here, never deceive anyone.) Lead in with something simple and straightforward: "Hi, Mr. Manager, this is Michael McIntyre and I am visiting with the Smiths today in Prairie View, Texas, just outside of Mule Shoe." Then go into a brief explanation of the prospect's question and wait for your lifeline's response. You may or may not already know the answer. Once you have received the answer, say, "Great. I thought that was it, but I wanted to make sure. Mr. Manager, I am going to put Mr. Prospect on the phone with you now, can you explain this to him as well?" Hand the phone to the prospect and say, "This is my manager, Mr. Jones. He would like to say hello to you." At this point, the prospect will take the phone and talk with your lifeline, after which your lifeline will tell the prospect that he wants to speak to you again. He will then give you any further coaching that you may need and hang up. Once this is done, go right back to your Five-Point Close if that seems necessary.

There are several important points to keep in mind, and most of them revolve around the key fact that you need to retain control of the situation. First and foremost, *never ask permission* to call your lifeline; the prospect may be reluctant to give it and you will lose control of the situation. Second, you should always have your cell phone with you and fully charged. If by some rare circumstance you have no service, simply say, "Excuse me, Mr. and Mrs. Prospect, I really need to make a toll-free call to answer your previous question. May I use your phone?" and proceed. Third, don't *ask* your prospect if they want to talk to your manager—they don't, so why ask? You must stay in control here; it is critical if you are going to help these people and make the sale.

After the prospect gives you back the phone, don't stay on for more than a minute or two. Stay on just long enough to get some quick coaching and to thank your manager in a professional manner. What happens if your client then says that they still want to think about it? The first thing you do is *agree with them.*

Earlier in the book I explained a little about my first trip to Wink, Texas. At that stage I was trained to call my manager or the home office if I got stuck or didn't understand something. So there I was, three hours into a classic presentation. The prospect had the money and the need, but they weren't going to do anything "right now." I didn't know the Five-Point Close at that time, but I did know to call my manager, which is what I did. The conversation went like this:

Me: Hi, Fred. This is Michael McIntyre and I am in the home of Mr. and Mrs. Prospect out here in Wink, Texas. Fred, I have explained to Mr. and Mrs. Prospect the benefits of the policy, but I thought you might be able to address their concerns.

Fred: What kind of concerns do they have?

Me: Well, Mr. Prospect doesn't want to do this now; he wants to think about it.

Fred: For Christ's sake, kid, what do you think I am, Houdini? Put him on the phone.

When I handed the phone to my prospect magic started to happen—within one minute my prospect was laughing and talking about his ranch and his cattle. I looked over at the wife and noticed that she was feeling a little left out, so I struck up a conversation with her about her grandchildren. We then proceeded to walk around the house looking at all her pictures while she told me about her family. We were gone for a good ten minutes, and when we came back to the kitchen table, Mr. Prospect was still on the phone. He handed it back to me, and Fred announced that the prospect was ready to buy now.

After agreeing to call Fred back later, I hung up the phone and turned my attention back to Mr. Prospect.

Me: All right, then. Let's get the paperwork started.

Mr. Prospect: Now hold on, Michael, I told you we weren't doing anything today.

Me: But you just spoke to my manager, and he said—

Mr. Prospect: Yes, he told the same damn lies you did and I ain't doing anything today!

So that was that. I left with my tail between my legs and a great lesson: sometimes you just cannot make the sale. So you say to yourself the same thing the barber always says— *"Next!"*—and move on.

Lifelines do work—maybe not 100 percent of the time, but most of the time they do. They will help you make a lot more sales than if you were working without them. Train your people to use them, and make sure your home office knows how to receive them. Practice, train, and promote lifelines; they work the great majority of the time.

Magic Buying Statements

When it comes to selling, listening is just as important as talking. If you truly listen to your prospects, they will tell you how to sell them. "We are not buying anything today." "We're just looking." "I'm gathering information and I will get back to you." These are all huge buying (and I like to call them "magic") statements. They are magic because you will usually make a one-time-call sale when you hear these words. The reason people tell you these things is because they know they are buyers, and if you have a good product and they have a need, they *will* buy *now!* It's that simple.

Listen for related stories. For instance, if your prospect says, "I am worried about [fill in the blank]" or they give you family history, sometimes within that discourse they will explain to you what they actually need. You need to listen; in fact, you should take notes. It doesn't matter if you are selling cars, homes, insurance, clothing, or #2 pencils. *The prospect will tell you how to sell them if you listen.*

You also need to tell stories that relate to their situation. Say your prospect can't decide whether they want their new home to be on a golf course or on a tree-shaded cul-de-sac. Instead of listing the obvious advantages versus disadvantages—though there is nothing wrong with that—I like to share an anecdote of a similar situation that paints them directly into the story. They will then be able to visualize the story and project themselves into it, and they'll experience all the emotions that go with it and come to a decision.

Try something along these lines: "Mrs. Prospect, I had a couple similar to yourselves about a year ago, not quite as young as the two of you. They were faced with the same decision, and it helped them to interview people who lived on a golf course. There are pros and cons, obviously, but in the end, it was a matter of privacy for them. They felt the cul-de-sac would offer them the privacy they needed and they were willing to trade the great view to have that privacy. Now, if you're more interested in the great views and open spaces offered by a home on a golf course, and if the occasional golf ball through the window doesn't concern you, your choice is clear."

When buying something we really want, we have all imagined how it will make us feel or look, or what status it will give us, before we make a decision. Think about it. When we shop for clothes, we try on the pieces and look into the mirror to see if we like what we see. Does it make me look fat? Do I look younger? Do I look like an idiot? Either way, we project ourselves, make up what we look like in that outfit, and base our buying decision on that image.

If you sell something less tangible, such as an insurance policy, stock, or funeral service, you really must have stories that prospects can relate to themselves. If you are brand-new in sales, you need to look to your mentor or manager for help. Once you can share the relevant stories, you will make more sales from their magic words.

One of the most important magic buying statements is when the prospects look at each other and say, "What do you think?" Now, this can only happen if you are making a presentation to two people. It could be a husband and a wife, a parent and an adult child, or any other combination of two people. Whatever the combination may be, when they ask those magic words, *don't say anything*. Just be quiet and listen. You will make the sale; it *will* happen.

Most of us know our weaknesses, and that's why we will tell people about them—that in itself is also a weakness. If a prospect tells you they aren't going to buy anything, it's because they know they are buyers. Look around—you will probably see a large vacuum cleaner, maybe new siding on the house, a fairly new car in the driveway, and a "No Solicitors" sign on the front door. They put up a defense because *they* know they tend to be buyers, and some salespeople fall victim to it. For the successful salesperson, these signs are great to see because they are *buying* signs. Look for them; listen for them.

Changing the Subject

You have given your presentation and your very best close (using, of course, the Five-Point Close) and you can see you're not getting anywhere. What do you do now? Change the subject. "So, Mrs. Prospect, how was your last trip to Philadelphia?" Or, "What do you think about [the latest headline in the local newspaper]? Or, "How is the new legislation going to affect your business?" There are hundreds of different "switch" topics to choose from.

Switching the topic is important because it gives you and your prospect time to rethink the deal. Sometimes a few moments of distraction from the "sale" will help clear the prospect's mind and allow them to think more clearly about your product or service without the "sales push." Being pushy turns people off. After a few minutes, you can easily segue back into your close and make the sale. Don't get frustrated—or at least, *don't show it.* Simply get off the topic for ten to thirty minutes, then come back and make the sale. You will be surprised at how quickly you will come up with different ideas. Chances are that your prospect will also look at your idea differently, allowing you to close the sale.

Many people say that this practice is great in theory, but in reality it is hard to make a one-call close. Sometimes that will be true; sometimes you will have to go back two, three, or four times before you close that deal. It might even take a year, but you could also make the sale *today.* Go in with a positive attitude, thinking that you are going to close the sale. If you don't make it, accept it and figure out what it is that you will have to do to close that sale the next time. Your chances of closing the sale today are no less than your chances of closing it next month or next year. It's all about your approach and your belief in yourself and your product.

In a sales profession, dealing with stress and frustration can be a challenge. Everyone handles these issues in various ways. A lot of people use exercise to do so. Whether you exercise in the morning to get yourself going or in the evening to relieve the stress of the day, you can use exercise as a time to clear your head and resolve any outstanding issues or problems that you have been thinking through. The solitary time to yourself and the physical activity combine to help you feel better able to deal with any issues that may be going on in your head or environment. Often they simply seem like smaller issues once you've stopped focusing on them for a few minutes.

nine

━━━━ ━━ ━━ ━━ ━━ ━━━━

After the Presentation

When is the appropriate time to follow up on a presentation? That all depends. If the client needs time to think it over, if you were getting more information, or if they wanted to get some testimonials, your follow-up time will vary. So let's take these scenarios one by one.

First let's say the prospect wants to think on it, talk it over with a trusted advisor, or look at their budget. I feel that no less than five business days is the appropriate waiting time in these cases. You should send a letter or an e-mail in the meantime, thanking them for their time and saying that you look forward to doing business with them.

If you are getting them more information, you'll want to contact them a bit more quickly. As long as it's not an hour after your presentation, of course—it should be at least one or two business days before you call back with the new information. Depending on what kind of product and proximity you have, try to set another appointment to get in front of them again. If you are communicating via telephone or e-mail, try to set an established time to discuss the new information. This will give you the client's undivided attention.

If you make the sale, don't contact the client until you're ready to deliver the product. However, you absolutely should drop a line saying that you appreciate their business in the days following that successful meeting. If someone is spending money with you, be appreciative, be sincere, but do not be a bother. No one likes to be patronized or gushed over. The other side of the spectrum is equally true; I have seen sale reps make the sale and never look back. This is a fatal mistake, especially if you're in it for the long haul. Your reputation and your word is truly all you have.

Whatever you do, follow up when you say you're going to follow up. Everyone understands that life does happen, and if your circumstances override your commitment, be sure to communicate with your prospect or client immediately and explain. *Never* take your customer for granted.

If you are making a callback for whatever reason, always assume the sale when you do make that call; nine times out of ten, you will get it. If you're calling your prospect, it should sound something like this: "Hi, Bill. This is Michael McIntyre. Hope all is well. I will be by tomorrow morning to finalize the paperwork if that works for you. Is that OK with you?" Or, "Hi, Bill, Michael McIntyre, how are you? I am good, thanks. I want you to know that we are ready to put in your order today; in fact, the reason I am calling is so I can place it now, and I will personally deliver it by Friday. Is Friday good for you?"

You get the picture. If they say, "Well, I still have to think about it," go through the Five-Point Close and make the sale—or at least set up a follow-up. Then drop another line saying that you wanted them to know that you totally understand their hesitation, want to assure them that this is the right decision, and will follow up by next week.

Part 4
Homework

_____ _____

Preparation is *key*. Use the checklist below to make sure that you're prepared, or use it as a basis for your own checklist.

Preparation:
- Get to the dry cleaner in plenty of time
- Polish those shoes (scuffed shoes or broken laces give a terrible first impression)
- Clean your car, inside and out
- Fully charge your phone and computer
- Pack chargers for your phone and computer, just in case
- Pack business cards (fresh and not bent), pens, and a notepad
- Have important addresses and phone numbers written down (technology can fail)
- Have your GPS charged and maps at hand
- Do a trial run to check on traffic and the route to the meeting
- Know alternate routes in case of traffic delays
- Have your materials, paperwork, catalogues, product samples, and so on packed
- Call the prospect's office to get a sense of how they answer the phone (are they abrupt, professional, courteous, friendly?)

- Test out the prospect's product if applicable (it's a great way to build rapport)

The best way to prepare for a presentation is to videotape yourself giving the presentation. It can be a little painful to watch but it will help you get a sense of how you're being perceived by the prospect. Notice what isn't working— bad posture, saying "um" or "ah," pauses, head bobbing, etc.—and work to tone down those elements or completely eliminate them. Continue to videotape yourself until you feel better about what you're seeing. The quality of the video is not important; use your cell phone if that's all you have handy. A low-tech way of doing this is to simply perform in front of a mirror. Watching yourself give the presentation will work just as well as recording it.

Part 5

After the Sale

ten

————— —— —— —— —————

Techniques for Getting More Sales

All right, you made the sale—great! You will notice that the moment you make the decision for the prospect and they agree with you, the energy in the room changes and so does your relationship. They have accepted you and they trust you. Your prospect has moved from a *potential* client to a *valued* client in an instant. If the mood had been heavy and serious, it will change to light and fun. Be careful at this point; don't count your chickens just yet. Remember that you need to be professional and be in the moment so that you do not fumble the ball. I like to remember the guy who celebrates his touchdown before he is in the end zone, then fumbles the ball on the one-yard line. A great many defeats have been snatched from the jaws of victory by salespeople who celebrate way too early.

Whether it's on a large sale or small sale, your first, second, or tenth sale of the year, you need to behave as if this is a routine matter. Don't be rushed. If you rush your client through signing before bolting out of the door to your next appointment, you do not look like you appreciate their time and business. Chances are that client will start to question your integrity and the decision they just made. Now, if the client says, "Hey, Michael, this has been a great couple of hours and we are pleased with our decision, but we have to get to church," then that's a horse of a different color.

After you make the sale and all the paperwork is done or the order has been placed, sit and visit for a little while. Talk about anything except the transaction that just happened, unless they bring it up. Enjoy their company and share some light moments. Stay professional and be courteous. We call this the "cool-down phase" and it should take thirty to sixty minutes. You can get another cup of coffee; if they offer you a snack, take it (again, don't drink alcohol or smoke). In general just relax with your new client. Look at the family pictures, take a tour of the farm, or check out their stamp collection. Establish a good relationship. Remember the little things. They will be very important when you send your "Thank you for your business" letter. Listen and look for signs. If they want to visit a little bit, then visit; if they want you to leave so that they can get on with their day, then make your exit.

When and How to Get Referrals

Don't ask for referrals at this point. Even though some salespeople think that right after you make the sale is the best time to do so, I disagree. It is much better to do so after the product/service is realized and they have seen you and your company do what was promised.

For my first ten years in sales, I didn't get any referrals. I sold to the people I had leads on and that was it. I did, however, often make multiple sales during one appointment.

I would make a sale and then the client would say something like, "Hey, I want my brother to get this." Often I would make presentations with extended family and friends present and sell to them as well. I was a lead hound. I cut my teeth on leads and I had to have them. I learned how to create leads and that was what worked for me.

Only once I began my own company did I learn how to get referrals. I recruited the best and most talented people, who taught me the power of referrals, and once we started, the results were amazing. It is possible to ask for a referral without imposing; timing is everything. We train our people to ask a new client only after the sale is buttoned up and the policy has been delivered or the service has been performed. After all, in this day and age, people want to know that they are recommending a quality product to their friends, family, and coworkers, and often they will only do so after trying it out for themselves.

Knowing how to ask is also of importance. Do not ask a question that is too broad—when people start thinking widely, they cannot focus and their mind goes all over the place. For example, if someone asks you for your favorite movie of all time, you might be a bit overwhelmed. If they break it down in smaller bites—"What is your favorite war movie made in the past ten years?"—you can probably name a couple fairly easily. The same thing applies when asking for referrals. Try phrasing your question like this: "Mr. Client, let me call on one of your golfing buddies so I can share this product with them as well. Who do you think that might be?" Or, "Mrs. Client, I know you have some friends in your bridge club who would really benefit from this service. Give me a couple of names and I'll be sure to make you the hero." It could be a Bible study group, a chess club, or country club—anything that puts their contacts into a category or compartment in their brain for easy access. You will get referrals—good ones.

When you do receive referrals, tell your client how and when you will contact them. Be clear on what is OK to share with the referral. Some prospects are very sensitive about what information they are willing to share. If you make a sale from a client's referral you should send a thank you note along with a nice gesture, such as a plant or a gift certificate to an appropriate restaurant. Remember—dare to be different! You are in the people business; be good to the people.

eleven

—— — — — ——

The Three *C*s of Selling

*S*ee the people, *see* the people, and then *see* the people! You must be in front of prospects. Without a doubt, you cannot make a sale unless you're in front of your prospect. You may be on the phone, on the Internet, or in their kitchen, but regardless of how you get there, you *must* see the people. You must have their attention.

In your sales career you may get discouraged from time to time. It may even seem like you *are* seeing the people but nobody is buying. Depending on what you're selling, one sale can make your week or even your month. Whatever the case may be, you need to clearly know your goals and how you can reach them.

Let's suppose your goal is to make $2,000 each week, and let's say that you generally close between 30 percent and 40 percent of your sales. Make the law of numbers work in your favor and break it down. If you need to hit that $2,000 per week goal and you normally see about ten people in a week, or at least have ten appointments or contacts, then visualize in your mind that when you see a prospect—whether or not you sell them—you just made two hundred dollars. In order to hit your goal, *you must see the people.* You need to be creative and persistent and see ten people that week.

It's not often that you know in advance that you will close a sale. Regardless, every sales call deserves your very best presentation, no matter what. If they buy, great! You made money. If they don't buy, you still made money. This way you may get to yes early in the week, your yeses could be sprinkled throughout the week, or it may be your last call of the week. We really never know. Use the law of numbers: the more people you see, the more likely you will be to make a sale. So take the noes in stride and keep going. Sometimes you must go through the weeds to get to the flowers.

Some salespeople think they know a good lead from a bad one or a good appointment from a not-so-good one— no way! You may get lucky or develop a pattern, but this is a dangerous assumption; just when you think you have figured out how to "game the system," fate, the economy, or some other element beyond your control will teach you that you can't actually game the system.

You can definitely make the odds better by practicing, getting coaching, going to training seminars, reading, and getting out there and doing your job, but unless you're Carnac or the Amazing Kreskin, you need to trust and rely on the law of numbers. You have to see the people. We all get the easy sales every now and then, but you will not make a living on them.

"The harder I work, the luckier I get." I like that phrase. It's the law of numbers. But if you are missing the three Cs and you don't have *enough* numbers, this is where your entrepreneurial skills come in. Figure it out, ask questions, use your brain, and create opportunities.

In 1993 I was rapidly expanding my annuity agency and was in Little Rock, Arkansas, opening another office for our company, all the while running appointments to make sales because I wasn't earning a salary. I didn't make a sale, I was out of leads, and it was a new area, so I didn't have an inventory. I was selling insurance to the senior market (clients over the age of sixty), so I opened the white pages and wrote down 199 names that were common in that age bracket, along with their associated addresses and phone numbers. I looked for names such as Richard, William, Emma, Mary, Elizabeth, and so on—and then I started to make calls. Within four hours I had made six appointments for the following two days. I went on to sell two policies and make my week, not to mention opening an office and proving that there were sales possibilities in Little Rock. It was my first time back there since my days in the air force, and Little Rock felt very different as a place of opportunity rather than as a military base.

With today's Internet and hundreds of ways to get leads and prospects, you should never be at a loss for the three Cs. Just *see the people*; tell your story ten times and you will make your goal. In fact you will surpass it most of the time, especially after you have been with the same company, product, or service for a while and know what questions people will ask or what objections they will raise. You will have the upper hand because you already know the answers.

In addition to the three Cs of selling, there are two more Cs that must be brought to light. First you have your little *c* that represents circumstances. Your car breaks down, your child gets sick, or a check you wrote to the church bounces. There are terrible traffic jams or snowstorms or perhaps your credit card is declined. There are a lot of circumstances that call for our attention, but for the most part they can be overridden by the big *C*—commitment. This big *C* is larger and more important than any circumstance. Commitment will overcome insurmountable odds; maybe not with one bounce, maybe it will take two large bounces and a hoop jump or two, but commitment can and will override most circumstances.

Most of us allow circumstances to become our big *C* and override our commitment. This is a major mistake. When you focus on the circumstances instead of victory you are already losing the battle. As we all know, whatever we focus on becomes the most important thing to us; in fact, it can become all we have. That's why it is so important that you focus on your commitment. That commitment doesn't have to be sales; it could be anything. But in this book, the focus is on sales—making the appointment and making the sale. Many salespeople fixate on the small picture of the circumstances rather than focusing on the larger picture: the game and reaching their goal. To be a successful salesperson you must focus on the larger picture. If you are having problems with commitment, try this: write down all of your goals and the things you wish to accomplish and then commit to making that happen. Promise yourself that you will make it happen *no matter what*. The small *c* of circumstance is just that—small.

The moral of the story is to get out and *see* the people. You will increase your chances as you increase your contacts and the number of presentations you make. Keep track of this on a weekly basis. You must measure your progress. This will help you track your successes and encourage you to continue. If you have a dip in sales you will be able to attribute it to a lack of contacts. You will also need to allow yourself some "spooling up" time. It usually takes around three or four weeks before you start to see results, but in ninety days you'll think, *Wow! This really works!* Stick to it and you will see!

Part 5
Homework

_____ _____

List the three Cs of selling:

1. _____

2. _____

3. _____

Name two additional elements of selling that begin with C:

1. C_____

2. C_____

The best referrals come from your own customers—people who are already sold on the product. Ask your customers if you can use them as a referral source. Be specific and don't be afraid to ask.

As you go about filling up your funnel with leads, ask yourself the following questions:

1. Who is my ideal client or customer?

2. How do I identify them?

3. How do I find them?

4. Who do I know who is going after the same types of leads but is not my competition?

5.   How do I liaise with them to maximize my efforts?

6.   How do I get referrals from them?

Use these questions to keep your sales funnel full of quality leads. *Now get out there and get selling!*

epilogue

———— —— —— —— ————

Seven Secrets for Success

It seems the number seven is a magic number. Recently I was strolling through Barnes and Noble and I saw *The 7 Habits of Highly Successful People*, *The 7: Seven Wonders That Will Change Your Life*, and *The Seven Principles for Making Marriage Work*.

While I still love having only five points in the Five-Point Close and believe that the Five-Point Close will allow you to be more successful than ever before, I also want to offer you seven keys to success that I have found to be exceedingly important in the success of a salesperson. These seven key items have helped me get to where I am today.

Use these seven tips as guidelines to help you reach your goals. Write each one down on a three-by-five card along with a line or two that inspires you or at least reminds you of that particular key. Together, all seven create the big picture of your success.

1. Take Responsibility

Own it. You are where you are because of the choices you have made throughout your life, no matter what they are or where you are. Whatever has happened to you is all because of you. Moving to Texas was a direct result of my decision to join the military rather than go straight to college. My wife and I married young. I went into the insurance business in an unconventional way. All of these choices brought me to where I am today. Take ownership of your circumstances and your life. We make a choice and then deal with the consequences—good or bad—of that decision. In the end, we learn from everything we do. If we are smart, we take that knowledge and apply it to the things that we do in the future so that we do not make the same mistake more than once.

When someone says something like, "My husband is such a jerk. He is not faithful and he is not a good father," or lodges some other complaint and acts surprised by all of this, I find the whole situation astounding. In my experience, people often go into denial when it comes to these issues. We choose to ignore the hints of a person's true personality or act like something didn't happen—especially early in the relationship—because we want that relationship to succeed, even if it has a rocky foundation as a base. In our minds we make everything out to be roses and rainbows. We marry the less-than-ideal person, settle, and have children with them, and then when things go from bad to worse, we whine, "Why me?" Why you? It is because *you* made those choices.

No one likes to admit to mistakes; it's not easy to take on our bad decisions and own them, but the sooner you do, the more quickly you can move on and start taking responsibly for everything that happens to you—learn from your mistakes so you can succeed. This is not only important in your relationships; it is also important to your sales career. The next time you have a poor prospect, a no-show, a difficult client, a great sale, a bonus, or a rediscovery of the power of the Five-Point Close, remember you chose *all* of it, consciously or unconsciously. Own the situation, learn, and win. The old saying still applies: if life gives you lemons, make lemonade!

During Bill Clinton's 1991 State of the Union address, he held up something that resembled a credit card—it was a "universal national health insurance card." Everyone thought, *Wow!* Of course, my reaction was slightly different. I was knee-deep in the health insurance business, selling to self-employed small business owners and doing very well— at least I had been. It didn't take long for everyone to start saying, "No thanks, Michael. I'll wait until the government comes out with its plan." The company I was representing lost its financing and the state took it over, which meant I needed to find a new deal.

I met with my father-in-law and we came up with a new marketing plan. It was a good one, but we were a little short on money so we started the old-fashioned way: using credit cards and the "float." Sales started rolling in and things were moving. We really didn't know what we were doing, but we did have good timing. Another huge insurance agency that we were both associated with had just gone under, and we knew almost all of the agents. Less than six months later, Jack suddenly died at the age of fifty-three.

Jack and I had worked closely for the previous six months, spending twelve- to eighteen-hour days together, traveling, and building the business. Jack was a great dealmaker and a legend in the business; he taught me so much over the years. He was not only my father-in law and my business partner, he was a mentor, a coach, a friend, and a real father to me. I don't think things had turned out the way he wanted them to, but Jack was a responsible man. He raised his two children after his wife left them. He loved them and really didn't want his daughter to marry a salesman. I think he wanted her to have a stable, normal life, and he understood that sales could be anything but stable.

The week following Jack's death was thick with emotions and an overwhelming sense of responsibility. I had been running the day-to-day business operations anyway, dealing with the banks, vendors, attorneys, and employees, but I was thirty-one years old and my business partner and mentor had just died. The responsibility for our new venture fell to me. After the funeral, I assembled all of my managers. I wanted to assure everyone that it was going to be OK, that I could handle this—which I did. But as I mentioned previously, just two weeks after we buried Jack, the whole house came tumbling down around my ears. That was when I *really* found out about responsibility.

Responsibility is a choice; either you take it or leave it. If you are going to be a success in any sales position, no matter if you're on straight commission or salary, you must be responsible for your success. Look in the mirror and know that *if it's to be, it's up to me!*

2. Learn and Learn Some More

My mentor taught me the importance of reading the newspaper every day. *USA Today, The Wall Street Journal,* the local paper, and industry periodicals help me stay in touch with my profession and enable me to speak about current events, which is very important. You don't have to read every page, but at the very least, you should scan every headline—these days it is even easier to do so with the Internet. I get tremendous ideas from the news and great third-party endorsements for things I am selling. Knowledge will always bring you credibility, and a tidy notebook in which relevant newspaper articles are pasted can be used to strengthen your presentation. Highlight key parts of the articles. Ensure the articles are current (from the last couple of months or years, depending on the life cycle of your product). Using articles that are outdated is counterproductive.

If you want to make a great income in sales, you *must* keep learning. If you don't, not only will you become bored, you will also bore your prospects and your sales will suffer.

Learn from Other People's Experiences
Determined to learn everything I could about sales, I spoke with my dad; after all, he is an insurance agent as well. He taught me "the power of the pen" and showed me some great closes. I was fortunate enough to be born with talents that I could leverage to create my success, but when things weren't going well I really struggled—until I learned the Five-Point Close. With that and constant continuing education, you will succeed.

Continue Your Education
Earlier I told the story of the awe I felt upon receiving my first check after my first week in the insurance business. It dawned on me years later that we salespeople have the

potential to make a very large amount of money compared to those in professions that require years of postgraduate education. Take medicine for example. The average medical doctor in the United States earns around $145,000, and with a specialty they can make a tremendous amount of money—up to $2 million a year in extreme cases. Yet the average physician makes much less, even though he or she still has eight years of postgraduate study and two to four years in an internship (at which time they earn about $40,000 annually) under their belt. When they finally go into practice they have to go deeper in debt on top of the hundreds of thousands of dollars they have in student loans from medical school. Doctors have to ensure that they are continually on the top of their game, and that means utilizing continuing education to stay abreast of new developments, technology, and studies. This is the only way for them to effectively treat their patients and be successful.

As a sales professional, with very little investment and not a tremendous amount of formal education, you can make a six-figure income—if you're willing to pay the price. The price is to learn your business and to read, read, and read some more. Study your profession. Go to classes, work with successful people in your field, network, and ask questions. We can all get lucky every now and then, but to make a great living in sales, you must keep *learning your profession.*

Do It Now

Procrastination is the downfall of many great salespeople. You may feel that everything has to be just so before you start. Perhaps you fear failure, rejection, or change. Maybe it's just good old-fashioned laziness. Whatever it is, you need to walk through it and *go.* In most cases, the timing will never be just right. Action breeds action: when you see the opportunity, just go for it!

When we are young we always believe that we have it all figured out. In my case, I believed that I would get out of the air force, go to State Farm, let them know who my dad was, and the doors would swing open for me. When I was honorably discharged from the military, I went to the district office of State Farm in Dallas. They said, "Well, son, if you want to be a State Farm agent, you really need at least fifty thousand dollars, an office, a property and casualty license, and to be able to make no money for about two years." That wasn't at all what I had imagined. Instead I found a different approach; I still didn't have money or even transportation, but I did it anyway.

More often than not the situation will not be perfect, so be flexible—have an open mind and get started. If you fail, so what? You will not be successful 100 percent of the time. Do it anyway. You have heard the saying, "Go with the flow." That's great advice whether you are starting a new job or company, launching a new product or ad campaign, or even wooing a new client. Whatever it is, do *not* get bogged down in the details. We all make up reasons for why things won't work, or we focus on the negative instead of going out there and stepping into the gap. If you are inflexible, your wallet will be equally inflexible in its emptiness.

3. Step into the Gap

The gap is a unique place, metaphorically speaking. We all have our comfort zones and most us never want to leave them. It's scary to do so, and we associate those scary feelings with something from our pasts—usually a negative experience—and we don't want to return to that place where we are not in control.

The problem is that when we're isolated in our comfortable box, we also get stale and obsolete, and we don't go anywhere except where we've already been. We stagnate. When we do something new, strange, adventurous, and even a bit scary, we step into the gap—the space before we get our footing, before we familiarize ourselves with the new or even understand it. The gap is where we feel young and adventurous. We also feel fear, vulnerability, excitement, and exhilaration. A whole range of emotions can come up in the gap. It is where you can make a difference, learn, and pave your path to success.

Do It Anyway

What makes one person more successful than any other is not education, good looks, or money; it is not even contacts or networking or great ideas. It is that successful people will *do the things that they don't like to do.* I don't like leaving my family on a Sunday afternoon to fly off on a three-day business trip, but I do it because that is the way that I can ensure that my family leads the life that I want them to be able to lead. I don't like having to spend hundreds of thousands of dollars on leads and postage, not knowing if it will pay off, but I do it because that is the way I believe will make money.

People who are not successful have no desire to get up early in the morning, so they don't. They don't like to work on the weekends and sacrifice their family time, so they don't. They certainly don't like to put their money on the line for an unsure thing, so they don't take the risk. They stay in their box and complain (for the most part) about how things are bad or how they wish they could find the "right deal" or the "good leads." Unsuccessful people basically *choose* to be unsuccessful; they get to be right (in their minds) and they stay frozen.

Write this statement down, as corny as it sounds. "If it's to be, it's up to me." Go for it! Yes, you'll feel your heart thump, you'll get butterflies, and you'll feel insecure at times. That's great! You are *feeling*! You are alive and making something happen. Yes, you may fall, but you'll get back up and do what other successful people do: do it anyway!

4. Come from the Heart

Some of you are thinking, *Oh no, not the touchy-feely stuff.* Let's put it this way: do you want to help people? It really is that basic. As humans we are emotional beings. If you exercise your heart a little, it will go a long way for you and the people you come in contact with. We can only come from two places: either the heart (love) or the ego (fear). Experience shows that when a person acts from their ego—that is, from fear—the situation generally does not turn out the way that they want it to turn out.

When Ego Rules

When I bought my first new car, I was extremely proud; however, being the perfectionist that I am, I quickly noticed that the car had a few minor flaws. Nothing of grand scale but important to me. I took the car in, gave them the punch list, and said I would pick it up the following week. I went back to get the car and everything had been done except for one little paint chip that wasn't touched up as well as I thought it should be. Here enters ego. I made a spectacle of myself. I was afraid that little chip would hurt my resale on the car, which brought up insecurities of being without. This is a bit frivolous, but ego-fear can and does show up in different ways, and it can seriously undermine any point or sale that you are trying to make.

Be a Good Samaritan

At one point in my career I did a ninety-day leadership training program. For our first project we were instructed to feed at least 250 homeless people. We were to provide the food and use the kitchen facilities and a small cafeteria in a downtown Dallas mission building to serve everyone. The catch was that we had only two hours to prepare to feed those 250 people, and we couldn't use any of our own money; we had to have the food *donated*. This was easier said than done. Most people refused our request, as we were not affiliated with an official organization. We were just thirty people trying to feed some hungry folks that day. I decided to accept my vulnerability and go to the local hotels to ask for help. We went to the chef at a local yet well-known hotel and explained exactly what we were doing. He gave us tons of food—enough for about 150 people. The other group went to a very upscale (and charitable) restaurant that donated the rest.

When we finally got to the mission and had everything set up, we didn't have enough people to feed! The majority of the homeless population was on the other side of town, so two of us drove our cars to pick them up. We both had rather nice, new cars, so when we got there the people were a bit leery. We explained we had a great hot meal for them and wanted to drive them over to enjoy it. I put five people in my car; then I looked at them and I got scared. I took a deep breath and said, "Gentlemen, this is really different for me, and to be honest with you, I'm nervous." The fellow in the front seat looked at me and said "Man, *you're* nervous? I am, too. I've never ridden in a Mercedes before." After that I was fine; we laughed and they enjoyed the five-minute car ride. I did about fifteen trips back and forth. I had to come from the heart and tell them how I felt; when I did, it was awesome. We fed the people and they were really appreciative. I was grateful for the experience and the privilege of giving. All of that only happened once I let my actions come from my heart and not from my ego.

Humans like to believe that we are all fallible and that no one person is better than another. You have to be real, be authentic, and be sincere. If you are fake or try to put on a façade, most people will see through it rather quickly, and you will have lost it all right then. No one believes or likes perfection in their fellow human beings.

I'm Here to Help

When you are giving a presentation, you *must* come with the attitude, "I am here to help you, not hurt you." Then you will always do right by the client. If you are thinking about your commission, you transition into fear and the "lack" or "need mentality." This will translate into your presentation. Try not to think about money and train yourself to focus on the prospect's needs, not your own; this will really benefit your financial situation in the long run.

Tell the Truth

Always tell the truth. This is all about integrity and coming from the heart. Many of us are afraid of the truth—don't be. If there is a negative perception of some sort about your product, bring it to the prospect's attention first—do not let *them* ask *you* to explain the negatives of your service or products. No product is perfect for everyone, so be honest and straightforward; most of the time the prospect will already know anyway. By being straightforward in your presentation you gain creditability in the eyes of your prospect.

Don't be afraid of the truth, as the truth will allow you to succeed in the long run. "The truth will set you free." That old adage is true. Once you embrace the power of the truth, you will be free to make more sales, free to keep your sales on the books, and free of debt as well.

5. Dare to be Different

If you are making a presentation to a couple that has been married for more than twenty-five years, chances are they have seen several hundred presentations of one kind or another. The people who pay attention usually know more closes than the closer. You must be different. How? Be creative!

If you are giving presentations to baby boomers or seniors and you are going to their home, never go empty-handed. You can go to any farmers' market and pick up fresh produce for next to nothing. Get some cloth bags or nice paper bags with handles and carry your gift with you to the door. When the client opens the door, take one step back, wipe your feet, and say something like, "Hello, Mr. Prospect, my name is Michael McIntyre and my wife and I thought you might like some fresh fruit and vegetables today." You will be amazed at the barriers that come down.

This homespun element separates you from the others instantly! Even though the prospect may not act like they care or may even be rude, don't worry—know that the last salesperson they saw didn't do this.

When you first meet your prospect, you have all of about fifteen seconds to make a lasting impression. When you show up bearing gifts it changes everything. You stand out—in a good way. This is a good start, but you need to *continue* to be different. Before you get there, do your homework about the prospect. Even if you have only their name and address, you can find out more about them through the Internet. For instance, you can get a rough idea of the value of their house through public tax records.

Some sales reps go to specialty advertising sources and get items such as pens, pencils, or magnets with their name on them to leave with the prospect or client. In the business we call these items "trinkets and trash." Your job is to make the prospect feel special, not to feed your own ego. You could create a nice notebook for the prospect with their name, that day's date, your name, and the address of the meeting place printed on the front, containing blank pieces of paper bound with a saddle stitch. This lets your prospect know that you are professional and have your act together.

After your appointment, immediately take a few notes about your client or prospect. Record any milestones such as a big promotion, their thirtieth wedding anniversary, or their first grandchild, as well as any interesting discussions you had. Whatever it might be, remembering those details later will show that you were listening to them attentively.

Get a box of note cards—nothing pretentious, just a classic style—and at the end of the day, send them a note with something simple and customized written inside. For example:

Dear Mr. and Mrs. Prospect,

It was a pleasure to visit with you today. I am pleased to be of service to you for your financial needs. Congratulations once again on the birth of your grandson, William. I know you are very proud and blessed. I enjoyed our visit and will be in contact with you in the near future.

—Sincerely, Michael McIntyre

If you mail your note the next morning, they will receive it in about two days. Once again, this little detail sets you apart from rest of the group. It's all about differentiation.

To further distinguish yourself, tell people up front what you expect with a clear statement: "Mr. and Mrs. Prospect, I am glad to be here today. I am going to give you a thorough presentation, and I want you to give me a yes or no afterward. I know you may wish to think about it or visit with your advisors; however, the only thing I am requesting is that if it all checks out, I get a yes or no. Is that fair?"

At first this may be uncomfortable for some of you, but if you are traveling and don't want to stay over to make a call-back, try it. It has worked for me. Of course, I still would have gone back a time or two, but this way they knew I meant business. They seemed to pay closer attention and respect my time as well.

Another "different" thing you can do is pick up a *USA Today* newspaper to take to your prospect. Most people do not subscribe to *USA Today*, so it's a nice little touch. The paper is easy to read and entertaining as well.

6. Forgive

We tend to criticize many things and we get into the habit of making judgments. The harder—but much more beneficial—option is to forgive others.

You are probably wondering how this will help you with the Five-Point Close or even with selling in general. Let me tell you, if you are carrying around emotional baggage of any kind, it will affect you and your performance as a sales professional. It will also affect you in your relationships as a parent, manager, spouse, friend, or sibling. To forgive is much easier said than done; however, with practice you will master it. You will begin to catch yourself making judgments, creating grudges, or criticizing something or someone. Remember, while you might be criticizing others, you are not perfect either. The Bible says in Matthew 7, "Do not judge so that you will not be judged."

Many of us have had a prospect who was less than pleasant or one who didn't buy despite a fantastic presentation. Or maybe you made the sale only to find out that the prospect cancelled the order the next day. We can get angry and shut down, or we can forgive and go on. That is why forgiveness is one of the secrets to success. How is anger going to help you succeed? If you take that negative attitude into your next appointment, you are losing before you even walk in the door. You have all heard the saying "Misery loves company." I promise you, it's bad company! Stay away from it. When someone hurts us (which, by the way, we control and allow), we want to hurt them back. We could stop talking to them, shun them, and be vindictive, but all of those actions are huge drains on our energy and are not in the least productive.

I can hear you protesting now: "Yeah, but Michael, he stole money from me, I have every right to be angry." OK, you want to be right? That's fine, be right. But if you forgive you get so much more—you get freedom. Freedom from anger, hurt, and pain. You gain the freedom to move on, to control your emotions, and to grow from the experience.

Forgive your company, your prospects, your clients, your family, and anyone else you think may have done you wrong. Do it every day; say it and practice it. Surround yourself with people who are optimistic and forgiving.

"It is better to soar with the eagles than to flap with the turkeys," as some old-timer put it. That old-timer had it right. If you can control it, do so, but if you can't, get over it and move on; your reaction is something that you *can* control.

7. Persevere

How many stories have we read about perseverance? We know the anecdotes, and we know them to be true. So why do we quit? We quit because *it is easier to quit than to go on when we are at the end of our rope.*

We all get discouraged and disappointed. It's normal to feel defeated sometimes. The key is to feel it and then *move on.* Over my many years in sales, I have probably quit at least two hundred times. "And this time I *mean* it!" I've said that probably one hundred times. For some it gives a temporary sense of comfort to say it, but they never act on it. Yes, the stress can mount up; this is when you must seriously look at yourself and go after it or quit and find a new profession. There is no room in this profession for people who do not actively go after what they want.

This is where our profession loses some of its best talent. The spouse will say, "Honey, why don't you go and get a real job?" Or "Sweetheart, you can go to work for my brother at the shop, and we'll get benefits as well." This is all fine. There is nothing wrong with getting a salary or an hourly wage for honest work. But if you want to make a deep six-figure income and you do not have a professional degree, your chances are a lot better in sales. And in order to be successful in sales, you must persevere at all costs.

Getting into the sales profession is not an easy task. Just like anything worth having, it takes work, dedication, and above all else, perseverance. Everyone seems to think they understand until it's crunch time. If it were easy, they'd pay you a $45,000 base with a small bonus, a company car, and an expense account. It's hard, but for the few who make it on straight commission, it is extremely lucrative.

There are some great sales jobs out there that do offer a salary plus bonus, and you can do quite well—but you still must persevere and perform. You will still have times when you want to quit. Go ahead and quit—just don't tell anybody that you did. Go watch a movie, go for a run, or go for a short drive and listen to some great music. Get the feeling out of your system and then get back to work.

Bibliography

Albom, Mitch. *Tuesdays with Morrie: An Old Man, a Young Man, and Life's Greatest Lesson.* New York: Broadway Books, 1997.

Johnson, Spencer. *Who Moved My Cheese?* New York: G. P. Putnam's Sons, 1998.

Lundin, Stephen. *Fish! A Remarkable Way to Boost Morale and Improve Results.* New York: Hyperion, 2000.

Ziglar, Zig. *Zig Ziglar's Secrets Of Closing The Sale.* New York: Berkley Trade, 1985.

About the Author

Michael McIntyre is a self-made man. Starting with his humble beginnings in Flint, Michigan, everything he's accomplished in life has been through hard work. He used his time in the air force to receive a college education. After his honorable discharge in 1982, he came to Dallas; by 1983 he was winning top sales awards. Michael couldn't ignore his entrepreneurial drive, so in 1987 he started his first agency and it rapidly became the number one health insurance agency in the entire country. In 1992 Michael started a new agency selling annuities. He took the agency from zero to number one nationally in its class, producing over $3 billion in annuities by 2007. In 2005 he founded Benefits America, where he currently serves as the president and CEO.

Michael is active in his community, several charitable foundations, Young Presidents Organizations, Executives In Action, and his church, Watermark Community Church.

Michael isn't all business; he has been happily married for over twenty-five years to his adoring wife, and he loves his three beautiful daughters. Michael quips that if living with four females doesn't teach you the art of sales, nothing will.